knows that his thought deserves more critical attention than it has yet received. His new book is therefore more a stimulus than a retrospect. It states the agenda for the next thirty years.

In the second place, Bethge proves the fertility of Bonhoeffer's ideas by relating them briefly to the churches under Communism and at greater length to South Africa. Based on lectures given at the University of Cape Town, and with a chapter by the South African theologian John de Gruchy, this book explores afresh some of the questions as urgent for a Christian under apartheid as for one under Nazism. How does the Christian ministry become credible in a church of integrity? What are true ecumenism and authentic theology? How is a Christian to choose between exile and involvement, between compromise and martyrdom?

While Bonhoeffer does not answer these questions for us, he demonstrates supremely in his own life and thought what the answers were for him in situations not unlike our own. Beyond the frontiers of his church and country, "Bonhoeffer is relevant for us because he confronts us with the uncomfortable question: 'Who is Jesus Christ *for us today?*' "

EBERHARD BETHGE edited several of Dietrich Bonhoeffer's posthumous works and authored the monumental and definitive study, *Dietrich Bonhoeffer: Man of Vision, Man of Courage.*

BONHOEFFER:
EXILE AND MARTYR

Bonhoeffer: Exile and Martyr

EBERHARD BETHGE

Edited and with an Essay by
JOHN W. DE GRUCHY

A Crossroad Book
THE SEABURY PRESS • NEW YORK

The Seabury Press
815 Second Avenue
New York, N.Y. 10017

Library of Congress Cataloging in Publication Data

Bethge, Eberhard, 1909-
  Bonhoeffer, exile and martyr.

  "A Crossroad book."
  Includes bibliographical references and index.
    1. Bonhoeffer, Dietrich, 1906-1945.   2. Christianity—South Africa.   I. De Gruchy, John W.
  II. Title.
  BX4827.B57B39   260'.968   75-33303
  ISBN 0-8164-1211-1

CONTENTS

AUTHOR'S PREFACE

These lectures on Bonhoeffer had already been partly drafted for presentation in Buenos Aires and São Leopoldo in South America when I received an invitation from the South African Council of Churches to visit South Africa in the autumn of 1973. I revised the lectures for this purpose, and then gave them in various centres throughout the Republic. They seemed to be timely and surprisingly relevant to those pastors, laymen and laywomen, and students who heard them, and each time they provoked lively discussions which I still vividly remember.

The person responsible for my invitation to visit South Africa was Dr John de Gruchy who was then the Director for Communications and Studies in the Council of Churches. Having written his doctoral thesis on Bonhoeffer's theology, John de Gruchy knew very well how effectively a theology which was never just a verbal exercise could speak to the theological and ecclesiastical situation in his own country, even if this theology had been produced in another situation thirty or forty years before. Our experience of the encounter between this theology and the South African realities is still very much with us, because it was an encounter with people, people who are struggling hard for the appropriate interpretation of their faith in Jesus Christ in their situation.

We are grateful to the South African Council of Churches for making this rich experience possible, and to John de Gruchy both for the part he played in arranging our visit and for taking so much trouble in turning our German sentences into readable English.

Rengsdorf　　　　　　　　　　　　　　　　EBERHARD BETHGE
October 1974

ACKNOWLEDGEMENTS

Grateful acknowledgement is made for permission to quote the following material: the poem 'Exile' by Marianne Leibholz, which appears in *The Bonhoeffers: Portrait of a Family* by Sabine Leibholz-Bonhoeffer, published by Sidgwick & Jackson, London, 1971; extracts from *Letters and Papers from Prison* by Dietrich Bonhoeffer, enlarged edition, copyright © 1953, 1967, 1971 by SCM Press Ltd, published by SCM Press, London, and The Macmillan Company, New York, 1971; and extracts from *Ethics* by Dietrich Bonhoeffer, second edition, © SCM Press Ltd 1955, published by SCM Press, London, and The Macmillan Company, New York, 1971.

EDITOR'S PREFACE

At the end of his visit to South Africa in 1972, Visser 't Hooft, former General Secretary of the World Council of Churches and a friend and ecumenical confidant of Dietrich Bonhoeffer, remarked to some of us over a coffee-table in Johannesburg, 'It's all a paradox!' He was reflecting, of course, on the South African situation, of which he was an astute, sympathetic and yet critical observer. A few months later another friend and very close confidant of Bonhoeffer's visited South Africa. *Bonhoeffer: Exile and Martyr* is one of the results of that visit. Another result was a growing conviction in my own mind that we do live in a paradoxical situation which is rather unique, and that Bonhoeffer's theology can help us understand the meaning and the implications of the Gospel in South Africa today. Encouraged by Eberhard Bethge, I have attempted to explore this possibility in an essay in this volume. In doing so, I must confess that it is all rather tentative, and that it is written from the perspective of a white South African, who is nevertheless, like many others, concerned about the creation of a more just society. Indeed, the paradoxical nature of our society has become increasingly apparent during the past few months as the face of southern Africa has begun to undergo radical change, with South Africa fulfilling a leading, if ambiguous, role in the process. Whether or not South Africa itself will change as much and as rapidly as many hope and pray remains to be seen.

The essays 'The Dilemma of Exile' and 'Modern Martyrdom' were originally published in *Ohnmacht und Mündigkeit* (1969) by Chr. Kaiser Verlag in Munich. They have been shortened in translation. The appendix on 'A Confessing Church in South Africa?' (which highlights the paradoxical nature of the situation) is part of Bethge's report on his visit, originally published in *Evangelische Kommentare* (6 June 1973) and translated by the Publications Office of the World Council of Churches. It has subsequently been edited. In acknowledging these sources, we would like to thank those responsible for enabling us to use them.

It is not an easy task to turn German theological sentences into plain man's English. This book has proved no exception. The original translation was never intended for publication but for public lectures. Dr Käthe Gregor Smith, Mrs Angela Koch ('Modern Martyrdom'), and Eberhard Bethge himself ('The Dilemma of Exile') undertook this task. However, in preparing the manuscript for publication a great number of linguistic and other editorial changes have been made, and I am entirely responsible for the final form. Where I have been successful in providing a clear and readable English text, I am more than indebted to the suggestions of Jocylen Dunstan, Augustine Shutte, and my wife, Isobel. In thanking them, I would also express my gratitude to Shaan Ellinghouse and Gloria Hare for typing, and re-typing, the manuscript.

Our warmest thanks are due to Eberhard Bethge and to his wife Renate for their warm friendship and help, and for giving themselves so readily and energetically to us, and also for permission to prepare these lectures for publication. We would also thank their church in the Rhineland and the South African Council of Churches for making the visit possible, and Pastor R. Brückner of the Christian Academy in Southern Africa and officials in the German Evangelical Church who provided a grant to enable us to prepare the manuscript for publication. Finally, we are grateful to Messrs Collins, and Lady Collins in particular, for all their help and encouragement.

University of Cape Town　　　　　　　　　　　JOHN DE GRUCHY
Christmas 1974

INTRODUCTION
The Response to Bonhoeffer

The Germany in which Dietrich Bonhoeffer lived, learnt, re-flected, taught, wrote and acted no longer exists. It has broken up, and the two parts, East and West, commemorated the twenty-fifth anniversary of his death in different ways.

The Churches in West Germany still enjoy the privileges which a state that is interested in the forces of stability grants those corporate bodies that had more or less proved themselves up to the time of the Nazis. The society of this same state, however, notes with interest every sign of the waning effect and influence of the Churches. A new and restless generation energetically questions the authenticity and relevance of these ancient bearers of tradition. In view of the danger that they might lose their privileges, the Churches react in various, even contradictory, ways. They either attempt to go ahead with their progressive theological teaching and social ethic; or they bolster up old positions by developing a so-called 'modern theology' of revolution; or else they form new, very orthodox, 'confessional movements', which, of course, appeal especially to church administrations!

For many in the West Bonhoeffer is a menace to Christian identity and a destroyer of the Lutheran doctrine of the two separate kingdoms of Church and State. His 'non-religious interpretation' is looked upon as one of the causes of a dangerous second Enlightenment, and his underground activity against Hitler as overstepping the legitimate boundaries of the Church's domain. At the few ceremonies which took place in the churches of West Germany in commemoration of his death on 9 April 1945, churchmen and preachers avoided this embarrassing problem by saying: 'Do not worry, in spite of everything – that is, in spite of Bonhoeffer's participation in the conspiracy against

Hitler, and in spite of his last theological utterances and formulations – he was a Christian and remained one.' Of course it is difficult for the Churches, in their privileged position in West Germany, to recognize and formulate the specific contribution Bonhoeffer has made, let alone integrate it into the life of the Churches. Bonhoeffer speaks from a situation in which those privileges had collapsed; but for the West German Churches as they are today, that stage has yet to come. For them the nineteen-thirties seem no more than an episode.

The position is different in East Germany, the so-called German Democratic Republic. There Bonhoeffer's death, and his fragmentary notes from Tegel prison, mark not only the end of an episode in secular and church history, but the irrevocable end of an epoch and the beginning of a new one. The point of departure is that the Church too has to pay for the guilt of the past, and has to abandon all those privileges and advantages which as an established pillar of social and political life it once enjoyed. Bonhoeffer is being seen, to an ever-growing degree, as encouraging the Church to accept this position and, from this starting-point, to conceive the meaning of the Christian faith afresh. 'Religionless Christianity' is no longer intellectually questioned about its conceptual problems; 'the world come of age' is no longer theologically suspect and disputable. Perhaps these ideas are accepted too uncritically, but they simply serve as a basis for thought and work, so that new forms of witness and mission may be found without any given privileges.

The twenty-fifth anniversary of Bonhoeffer's death was commemorated in East Germany in conferences where a truly amazing acquaintance with Bonhoeffer's letters from Tegel prison intensified the discussion to a rare degree. Christians in the Communist zone of Germany experience those fragmentary notes from prison not as something that might endanger their own identity, but on the contrary as helping them to realize it afresh. While in West Germany Bonhoeffer may be criticized for originating movements which lead to a cheap kind of adaptation to the world – 'a sell-out of spiritual substance', as it has been called – Christians in East Germany see a greater danger in their situation in the temptation to brick themselves up inside an ecclesiastical ghetto of defiance. It is from this danger that Bonhoeffer's insights deliver them – not because he thought through all their problems, they say, but because he pointed to the way whereby they can be thought through. 'The Church today must be "the Church for others" [one of Bonhoeffer's last, surprisingly simple, formulations], because those others exist' was one thesis of an East German conference, showing the starting-point and the direction.

In Western Europe the religious communities of Mirfield in England and Taizé in France celebrated the Eucharist of Christ *'ressuscité en communion avec son témoin fidèle Dietrich Bonhoeffer'*. But it seems that only with the publication of the biography of Dietrich Bonhoeffer in English[1] at that same time have English-speaking Christians come to realize the whole depth and bitter-ness of Bonhoeffer's involvement in the conspiracy against Hitler, with all its fearful consequences. The image of the saintly martyr which had been cultivated for twenty years now no longer fits. How could Bonhoeffer, with such an involvement, preserve his personal integrity, his integrity as a Christian and a minister of religion? This is the question asked by the news media. Indeed, it requires an effort of the mind to make us understand how, by taking this step, Bonhoeffer regained the integrity and freedom of a theologian, which had so often been endangered by the Nazis, and thus, and only thus, became the authentic witness.

While here in the West a middle-class Christian faith shrinks from recognizing this phenomenon in its clear outline, others in the East European world are just discovering it, though not without being tempted to mould it to their liking. Four years ago the Soviet Academy of Sciences in Moscow, in its monthly magazine *Voprosy Filizofii*,[2] introduced Bonhoeffer to its readers. In an essay called 'The Non-religious Christianity of Dietrich Bonhoeffer', D. Ugrinovic tried to show that Bonhoeffer, realizing that the Christian substance of faith had reached its end, transformed it into a purely immanent ethic. Ugrinovic does not ignore the fact that Bonhoeffer wanted to be a theologian and not just a moral philosopher, or in what way he wanted to be one, but he describes his theological ideas as uninteresting and nebulous. Somewhat related to this essay, and yet of a much greater depth, is a biography of Bonhoeffer and a collection of his writings published in Poland by the Roman Catholic writer, Anna Morawska of Krakow. In a private conversation she named the reasons for Bonhoeffer's ever-increasing importance for people of her persuasion in Poland:

Bonhoeffer is so exciting because he has dared to anticipate in thought our problem of how to meet Christ in a religionless world. Who are we, who, in the midst of atheism, do not wish to understand ourselves as agnostics, but feel veneration for Christ; how may we interpret our relation to Jesus? In Bonhoeffer we see somebody who might be able to help us when we feel that it is simply wrong to see the barriers dividing the so-called believers and the so-called unbelievers. Do not such barriers rather run right through the group of believers and that of unbelievers: namely, separating those who live for others from those who do not, whatever group they may belong to?

Towards the end of his life Bonhoeffer recognized the need for the incognito of the believer, a need conditioned by his Christian faith, and he lived up to it to the bitter end. He felt the frustration of modern man over against the great classical formulations of the Church, and the chasm lying between theological statements and the experiences of the layman. In fact, he experienced the barrier not in the realm of the Creed, but with ethics.

And then, in the history of Poland it has always been counted an honour – almost incomprehensible to citizens of the West – to be a conspirator and a prisoner. After all, Bonhoeffer, coming as he did from a middle-class situation and thus responsible for a great cultural heritage, was not prepared, unlike ourselves, for the great upheavals which were to follow. And yet, in that very capacity, he was ready for the great revision, being disappointed by the confessionalist attitude of his Church, averse to the great establishing systems of theologies and ethics, and interested in man who had to live on in a transformed future. That is why, far beyond the frontiers of his Church and his country, he does not belong to an episode, but to an epoch which he has helped to shape, just as he helped to shape and clarify our own understanding.

THE SOURCES AND THEIR INTERPRETATION

The history of how Bonhoeffer has been received and interpreted depends greatly on the way the sources have become known and translated. The appearance of the sources in its turn, however, has been determined by the ups and downs of the way the material has been received. Certain theological concepts of influential recipients such as the Bultmann school in Germany or the Death-of-God theologians abroad have influenced how the sources have become accessible. Some theologians, attracting much publicity, erected theses and structures on the basis of Bonhoeffer's letters, and even then on sometimes doubtful translations, before they were able to read important sections of Bonhoeffer's complete works in their own language. I myself am to blame for having been too complacent in allowing certain sensational theses like those of the Death-of-God theologians to pass uncriticized. I did so in the hope that those seriously interested in Bonhoeffer would soon discover their superficiality by getting to know all the writings. I have to admit, however, that the atmosphere in which works are received is always determined by those who know how to speak first, and to speak in a sensational manner, thus determining certain ways of posing questions and reacting to the sources. All the same, the most effective response was provoked by John Robinson's fascinatingly one-sided booklet *Honest to God*[3] and this introduced the most fruitful period for the study, translation and publication of all of Bonhoeffer's works in the Protestant, Roman Catholic and secular spheres.

Stage One

Bonhoeffer's first two, and from a scholarly point of view, most accomplished books, *Sanctorum Communio* (1930)[4] and *Act and Being* (1931),[5] were not a success during his lifetime. Hardly anybody read them, let alone adopted his position. Like other doctoral theses, they were hardly mentioned in the press. Only after the great success of *Letters and Papers from Prison*[6] did we discover their far-reaching and revolutionary insights. And it was only in 1955 that Karl Barth paid *Sanctorum Communio* the following tribute:

> [It] not only awakens respect for the breadth and depth of its insight as we look back to the existing situation, but makes far more instructive and stimulating and illuminating and genuinely edifying reading today than many of the more famous works which have since been written on the problem of the Church . . . I openly confess that I have misgivings whether I can even maintain the high level reached by Bonhoeffer . . . so many years ago.[7]

This tribute was, however, accompanied by Barth's advice to stick to Bonhoeffer's early and middle writings rather than to the prison letters, implying that we should learn more from the teacher of a Church *in* the world than from the teacher of a Church *for* the world, more from the fighter for the otherness of the Church than from the fighter for the 'Church for others'.

Since the fifties these two books have gone into several editions in German and English. At the moment almost more post-graduate students are working on these early writings than on the last fragments, and their rootedness in the nineteenth century fascinates scholars. These new studies stress different points according to the students' own interests. *Sanctorum Communio*, for example, is indeed being examined with regard to its ecclesiological aspects, but for some its sociological and anthropological elements are of great interest. In other words, scholars are interested in uncovering the early roots of the anthropological interest which dominates Bonhoeffer's last writings. Thus, some gaps in our knowledge are being filled, and fresh sources for understanding Bonhoeffer and his impact are being discovered.

Stage Two

It was a different matter with the main writings of Bonhoeffer's middle period, *The Cost of Discipleship* (1937)[8] and *Life Together* (1939),[9] for, from the outset, they were not really academic or specialized books. Written in a far more original and hence far more readable style, they attacked spiritual areas sacred to the Lutheran Church. They described fresh possibilities of existence for the Christian, claiming to lay open the true nature of re-formed and biblical teaching. A critical passion and the vision of a community-forming discipleship stirred interest not only among theologians and Christians of the Confessing Church in National-Socialist Germany, but also, after the war, in the English-speaking world, where an abridged edition of *The Cost of Discipleship* appeared in London in 1948, with a foreword by George Bell, Bishop of Chichester. This projected the first image of Bonhoeffer, namely, that of a man who takes the Sermon on the Mount seriously and who experiments in the name of costly grace against cheap grace. And thus the martyr was raised up to become a hero of faith and sanctity. This image has been accepted until today, as shown by the horrified reaction in London when the integrity of Bonhoeffer was later questioned. His report on the life of a German Protestant community in the thirties, *Life Together*, comes nearest of all his works to equalling the number of editions published, in Germany and elsewhere, of the letters from Tegel prison, and it has been translated into as many languages.

And yet the theological reception of these two books of this originally most effective period of Bonhoeffer's life quite clearly does not measure up to that accorded the works of his first and last periods. Their language and style are considered to be not sober enough and too didactic, and their form of piety is regarded as out of date. The general feeling of uncertainty or doubt about these books is supported by Bonhoeffer himself in a letter of

21 July 1944. Speaking of *The Cost of Discipleship*, he wrote the often quoted words: 'Today I can see the dangers of that book, though I still stand by what I wrote.'[10]

The first book on Bonhoeffer's theology to appear in German, by Hanfried Müller in 1961, is as brilliant as it is biased and interprets the period in which these books were written as a dead-end from the confines of which Bonhoeffer was at last liberated in prison.[11] Heinrich Ott's solid book, *Reality and Faith: The Theological Heritage of Dietrich Bonhoeffer*,[12] simply omits any mention of *The Cost of Discipleship* and *Life Together*. Among the thirty or so doctoral theses known to me, only two are specially devoted to the study of *The Cost of Discipleship* and the period when it was written, and these two are written by Roman Catholic scholars. Again, it was Karl Barth who expressed the highest praise for *The Cost of Discipleship* – though during Bonhoeffer's lifetime he never let him know how much he appreciated it, which would have meant a great deal to Bonhoeffer. In 1936 Bonhoeffer had written to Barth:

> The whole period was basically a constant, silent controversy with you, and so I had to keep silence for a while . . . I am engaged in a work on the subject and would have asked and learnt a very, very great deal from you.[13]

Barth later wrote in his *Church Dogmatics*:

> Easily the best that has been written on this subject [discipleship, sanctification, etc.] is to be found in *The Cost of Discipleship*, by Dietrich Bonhoeffer. We do not refer to all the parts . . . but to the opening sections . . . In these the matter is handled with such depth and precision that I am almost tempted simply to reproduce them in an extended quotation. For I cannot hope to say anything better on the subject than what is said here . . .[14]

But this praise too was uttered only after the first wave of enthusiasm about the prison letters had swept the country and annoyed Barth so much. When I was one of Bonhoeffer's students and a member of his seminary at Finkenwalde I heard him lecturing on discipleship, and these lectures formed my theological position as well as that of many others. From their perspective I was inclined to see everything that followed; later, when looking back on the previous period (a retrospection which had been occasioned by the prison letters), my judgement became more balanced.

Stage Three

For a long time I was not aware of what lay hidden in my desk in the form of those letters smuggled out of the Tegel prison cell in 1943 and 1944. It was six years before we dared to hand a selection of them to the publisher, without the slightest idea that they would produce such a wide and lasting effect. For Bonhoeffer himself had told me that he considered work on a new *Ethics* to be the task of his life. He had planned this at a time when dialectic theology had attacked all attempts to write on ethics at their very roots, thus making such an attempt very hard indeed. Bonhoeffer started four times; but owing to his arrest, the book was never finished. George Bell, Bishop of Chichester, knew of Bonhoeffer's work on it and after the war saw to it that I would be enabled to collect and edit the fragments (1949).[15] I arranged the existing chapters following a plan sketched out by Bonhoeffer during his early work on the *Ethics*. This turned out to be satisfactory as an artificial harmonizing of the different levels of development. Soon other works on ethics appeared, such as those by Söe, Elert and Thielicke, and these dominated the libraries and seminaries, whereas Bonhoeffer's *Ethics* had no resounding effect.

Meanwhile *Letters and Papers from Prison* stirred a general interest in Bonhoeffer, the first English translation appearing in 1955. In 1956 Ronald Gregor Smith published his book, *The New Man: Christianity and Man's Coming of Age*,[16] in which he took up Bonhoeffer's questions and formulations in the letters as an epoch-making turning-point; and in 1961 Hanfried Müller asserted Bonhoeffer's leap forward into an entirely new worldliness during his time in prison. Later John Robinson was to speak of 30 April 1944, the day on which the first letter containing the new formula of a 'religionless Christianity' was written, as a date to be compared with 30 October 1517, when Luther nailed his 95 theses on the cathedral door in Wittenberg. Only after the publication of these two books did I rearrange the contents of the *Ethics* in their chronological order (since its sixth edition). It now became possible to trace the line and process of thought from the *Cost of Discipleship* to the *Letters*, and that meant to the newly apprehended worldliness of the Gospel.

Bonhoeffer's *Ethics*, the writing of which he himself looked upon as the great task of his life, still seems to be his most neglected book. It is true that there are special problems, such as social ethics, which either are not mentioned at all, or seem to be dealt with in a rather too conservative fashion. Hanfried Müller regards the *Ethics* as an interim stage leading to what is essential in Bonhoeffer's thought. However Ronald Gregor Smith said, a short time before his death (and others now think like him), that he considered the *Ethics* as harbouring the greatest treasures, as yet almost undiscovered, of Bonhoeffer's thought. There is, for example, the variously formulated basic supposition that without Christ reality cannot be recognized and related to, and that without reality Christ cannot be recognized and obeyed.[17] The idea of the ultimate and the penultimate as expounded in the *Ethics* has been stressed as particularly fruitful by some scholars.[18] Heinrich Ott interprets the *Ethics* on the basis of its understanding of reality. Benjamin Reist[19] sees the *Ethics* as 'the cutting edge' of Bonhoeffer's theology, especially in its attack on thinking in two spheres; the chapter on 'what is meant by telling the truth?' he considers, morally and theologically, to be the most transparent one. Reist leans on Paul Lehmann, who regards his own *Ethics* as a new interpretation in the American field of research of Bonhoeffer's basic elements.[20]

Stage Four

It was only with the publication of *Letters and Papers from Prison* in the winter of 1951–2 that the way was prepared for a theological sensation, and by a book which Bonhoeffer had not intended to write, consisting as it does of excerpts from letters, with not more than fifty pages of theological reflection, and addressed as it is to a friend, not to the world in general. This book, as I said, has drawn a response which has still not died away.

Karl Barth repeatedly pointed out the slender basis for a new theological development in these letters, and others have done the same. He did so for the last time in a letter to me of 22 May 1967:

> It is unthinkable – and I put myself in his place now – what people would have done to me had I died a natural or violent death after the publication of the first or even the second *Epistle to the Romans* or after the appearance of my *Christliche Dogmatik im Entwurf* in 1927. What I would not have wanted to happen to me in such a case I would very much rather not have seen happening to Bonhoeffer.[21]

The first echoes, expressing surprise as well as agreement, came as early as 1951 from Gerhard Ebeling and Helmut Thielicke. Both of them felt encouraged by Bonhoeffer's thoughts, the former because of his own reflections on the language event of the Gospel, the latter because he wanted to base his own ethics on Christology. Ronald Gregor Smith, too, immediately recognized the force and necessity of Bonhoeffer's method of enquiry: in 1953 he published the letters in English, and a flood of new editions was subsequently published. Meanwhile *Letters and Papers from Prison* has become a 'classic'.

The publication of *Letters and Papers from Prison* had three immediate effects. Firstly, when it appeared in 1951–2, theological discussions were dominated by the second great wave of the debates on demythologizing. Bonhoeffer's slogan of 'non-religious interpretation' seemed to provide support for Bultmann's existential interpretation. This is indicated in Ebeling's essay, written in 1955, 'The Non-religious Interpretation of Biblical Concepts',[22] which has become famous as an excellent reflection on Bonhoeffer's letters from Tegel prison. In the *Festschrift* for Bultmann of 1964[23] G. Krause reproved me, and G. Harbsmeier even more forcefully,[24] for trying to interpret

Bonhoeffer's formulations on the basis of Barth, rather than in terms of Bultmann. Thus Bonhoeffer's last statements had little chance of being heard in their own right, caught up as they were in the Bultmann debate. His own specific contribution remained hidden.

In this situation, several former students and friends of Bonhoeffer met intermittently from 1954 onwards in order to examine in lectures and discussions Bonhoeffer's legacy considered on a wider basis than that of the prison letters alone. Thus the series *Die Mündige Welt* came into being, with a variety of contributions such as the two fine studies by Regin Prenter on the Bonhoeffer–Barth relationship[25] and the Bonhoeffer–Luther relationship,[26] or Moltmann's contribution, 'The Reality of the World and God's Concrete Commandment According to Dietrich Bonhoeffer'.[27] On the basis of this series, Ronald Gregor Smith published in 1967 a symposium in English entitled *World Come of Age*.[28]

The attempt to collect such essential contributions to the secondary literature in such a series had, however, to be abandoned after the fourth volume because, in the meanwhile, too vast a literature on Bonhoeffer, including many minor articles, had been published. The list so far shows more than five hundred articles. A fifth volume, however, has continued the series in a new form by publishing work done on the sources and research from archives. Thus in 1969 this fifth volume, edited by Jörgen Glenthoj, was published under the title 'Documents on Bonhoeffer Research 1928 to 1945', and it has meanwhile made an indispensable contribution to our knowledge of the life and times of Bonhoeffer.

The most lasting result of the early response to the *Letters and Papers from Prison* was the decision not only to republish Bonhoeffer's early books, which contain so many of his important formulations – thus bringing them to the general notice for the first time – but also to put at the reader's disposal, in the *Gesammelte Schriften*, the entire, otherwise inaccessible, collection of essays, unpublished writings, reconstructions of lectures (among them the specially important lectures on *Christology*[29] of 1933), letters, sermons, and other documents. The collected works comprise six volumes published between 1958 and 1974.[30] A selection of these has been published in English in three volumes entitled *No Rusty Swords, The Way to Freedom* and *True Patriotism*.[31]

The German edition is arranged in the following order: *Ecumenism* in the first volume, *Church Struggle* in the second, *Theology* in the third, and *Sermons* in the fourth. The fifth volume is based on newly found sources, including reconstructions of the lectures which were added to the German edition of the biography in an appendix. Volume six contains diaries, letters and other previously unpublished documents. This collection is bound to seem bewildering to the inexperienced reader, bearing as it does the marks of how it was compiled. Only after the first volume had appeared on the market did some people involved in Bonhoeffer's life and possessing certain sources open their desks and, by producing this material, force the editor to squeeze it in where it did not really belong! But a complete edition which has been planned for the future will observe a strict and satisfactory chronological order.

CONCLUSION

The first wave of interest in Bonhoeffer ebbed away with two comprehensive studies of his theology by H. Müller and John Godsey, the former brilliant, but exploiting Bonhoeffer's ideas in the interest of Marxism, the latter reliable, but over-cautious.[32] Typically, both of them were doctoral theses. William Hamilton was right in maintaining that professors did little work on Bonhoeffer, 'which is why there is such an astonishingly short list of books and articles on him, and an even shorter list of good books and articles'.[33] Was the state of the sources too unattractive and too confused? Had Bonhoeffer's place in theology been settled too quickly, perhaps in the Bultmann camp? Or was it supposed that he would not yield anything worth the trouble of finding

23

out? In this situation a fresh and surprisingly powerful wave of interest in Bonhoeffer began with John Robinson's *Honest to God*, an eclectic book which again placed Bonhoeffer alongside Bultmann, but even more with Paul Tillich. This new emphasis spread in a number of directions.

Under the impact of Robinson's book the English-speaking public did not take up the traditional German problem of exegetical interpretation (Bultmann), the 'non-religious interpretation', but debated 'religionless Christianity', a formula used much less by Bonhoeffer. It is not the problem of interpretation which comes to the fore, but the question of relevant forms and structures; in what way can a Christian and the Church live today without religion? How must we understand the structure of prayer, the liturgy, and the life of the congregation? The difference in the choice of formulae – 'non-religious interpretation' in Germany, and 'religionless Christianity' in the West – reveals a difference in tradition and hence a different concern. There is no doubt that Bonhoeffer was concerned about *both* the question of interpretation *and* that of the form of Christianity (*Gestalt*).

The most spectacular effect of the second wave of interest became apparent in the United States, where the Death-of-God theology made the headlines. In Germany this was received with reservations and only when the serious academic interest in it in America was already fading away. Wherever this movement referred to Bonhoeffer, and some theologians like Paul van Buren and William Hamilton for a certain period relied heavily on him, he was misinterpreted or misunderstood. Some even tampered with Bonhoeffer's thought, and with an insufficient knowledge of his work, did violence to or destroyed his dialectical way of expressing himself. What was happening was at least made clear by William Hamilton once, when in the course of a discussion he remarked, 'We make a creative misuse of Bonhoeffer!' It is thus obvious that in this movement we had to do with extremely arbitrary developments whose consequences are untrustworthy in interpreting Bonhoeffer. At the same time, however, Bonhoeffer's theology of the Cross does require a thorough study of the problem of the 'death of God'.

Strange to say, it was Robinson's book, with its sensational publicity, and the misuse the Death-of-God theologians made of Bonhoeffer which led many Roman Catholics to explore what it was that fascinated people about Bonhoeffer's thought. I have knowledge of at least eight doctoral theses written on him by Roman Catholics.[34]

After the publication in 1967 of my comprehensive and detailed biography of Bonhoeffer (translated into Dutch in 1968, into French in 1969, into English and Spanish in 1970, into Japanese in 1973, and into Italian in 1975), it looks as if the strong disparity between, on the one hand, a general interest in Bonhoeffer, as expressed in innumerable quotations, essays and references, and the scant result in really substantial studies, on the other, will gradually disappear. It is true that the impulses which Bonhoeffer felt have for a long time been amazingly and lastingly effective wherever Christian groups experiment in abandoning the privileged positions of the Church; but the comprehensive theological study and appraisement of his work is just beginning. Heinrich Ott, the only professor and head of a theological faculty who has so far devoted a fully-fledged book in the German language to the study of Bonhoeffer, begins his reflections with the statement that Bonhoeffer has to be looked upon as 'one of the most hope-inspiring figures, perhaps the most hope-inspiring figure, of modern Protestantism'.[35] The preliminary work needed to substantiate that statement has indeed gone far.

Bonhoeffer in South Africa

An Exploratory Essay by John W. de Gruchy

Unlike many contemporary German theologians and pastors, Dietrich Bonhoeffer never visited South Africa, nor does he mention South Africa in any of his extant writings. If he were still alive, it is very unlikely that he would have kept silent on South Africa, or refused an invitation to visit the country. But there is a sense in which he has visited us and spoken to our situation, both through his own writings and witness, and through his close friend and interpreter, Eberhard Bethge.

As we listened to Bethge's lectures on Bonhoeffer during his visit to South Africa in 1973, it became increasingly obvious how relevant Bonhoeffer's life and thought is for our situation today. Some laymen who attended a seminar on Bonhoeffer, but who had no previous knowledge of him, innocently enquired: 'When did Bonhoeffer visit South Africa? He knows our situation from the inside!' But few South Africans are really familiar with his words and deeds, and only some theologians and pastors have given serious attention to his theology and its contextual implications. Perhaps for some in Europe and North America, theology has now moved beyond Bonhoeffer, but we have only just begun to encounter him in South Africa. In 1965 Harvey Cox considered the question 'Beyond Bonhoeffer?', and concluded his essay by saying: 'Of course, Bonhoeffer has been misunderstood and misused. He will be again. Of course theological fads are always dangerous. But we are in no sense finished with Bonhoeffer. Nor do I believe we can move "beyond" him until we begin to be the kind of Church he knew we must be, a Church which lives on the border of unbelief, which speaks with pointed specificity to its age, which shapes its message and mission not for its own comfort but for the health and renewal of the world.'[1]

Bonhoeffer had the ability to be objective even within the extremely disturbing and difficult circumstances in which he lived, so that it can be said that his '*freedom* from time and place and circumstance' is an important factor in interpreting his thought.[2] His theological work was not eclectic or erratic, nor was it based on expediency, but it was concerned throughout with the reality of God's revelation in Jesus Christ. At the same time, while his theology has universal relevance because of this concern for God's revelation, it can only be fully understood in terms of its original context. His concern was for the concreteness of God's revelation in Christ today. Thus, his life, thought and times are inseparable. In other words, it would be wrong for us to try and import Bonhoeffer into our South African situation, and to attempt to make his theology indigenous. Indeed, to do so might even become a way of escape from the real issues, and from a genuine theological response to them. Though there are undoubted parallels between the situations he faced during his lifetime and the situations we encounter in our country today, no two historical situations can simply be equated. Our approach to Bonhoeffer in South Africa must be different, it must be based on Bonhoeffer's *approach* to his situation. Bonhoeffer is relevant for us because he confronts us with the uncomfortable question: 'Who is Jesus Christ *for us today*?' He does not answer the question for us, but he demonstrates in his own thought and supremely with his life what the right answer was for him in a variety of situations. Thus, both the question which he asks us, and the answers which he wrote with his pen and his life, confront us differently but inseparably. As we discern how he wrestled with Christian authenticity in his context may we be reminded of, and discover fresh implications for, Christian faith and obedience in our context.

Today we invariably read all that Bonhoeffer wrote in the light of his subsequent martyrdom, and therefore his words take on added power and significance. But like a true martyr, Bonhoeffer did not seek martyrdom; he pursued the truth as he saw it and was executed because he lived that truth. Nothing could be more relevant or demanding for us than this, but the cost of doing the truth may be more than we are prepared to pay. This is an essential part of the background against which we must read and reflect upon *Bonhoeffer: Exile and Martyr* in any situation. Many years before his death, Bonhoeffer wrote, 'When Christ calls a man, he bids him come and die.' But he went on to say that the call to discipleship means both death – and life.[3] Each person must respond to Bonhoeffer's final witness in the depths of his own soul. It is a costly witness, but it is a witness to life and hope.

The paradox of hope

Like many South Africans, Bonhoeffer spent a year of post-graduate theological study in the United States. In February 1933, after his return to Germany, he wrote to his American friend and teacher, Reinhold Niebuhr, and after complaining about the German paranoia over communism, he continued by saying:

> In our country one is unbelievably naïve. The way of the Church is darker than ever before. But since I left you, there has been considerable change in your situation, too. It cannot, however, be denied that we, especially here in Europe, live in a tremendously interesting time, and one would really not like to change it for another.[4]

These words sound very familiar. In spite of the difference between Bonhoeffer's situation and ours, they could easily have been written by a South African student after returning home from overseas, for so many return with new perception and discover that the land they love is unbelievably naïve. They also return anxious to discover whether or not there have been any significant changes in the situation during their absence. Some even confess that they are glad to be home, not just because it is home, and certainly not because they like the 'South African way of life', but because it is a tremendously challenging situation, and though they may be tempted to change it for another, they know that this is where they belong. Bonhoeffer would have understood; he was often tempted to leave Germany, and did so for short periods. Indeed, within six years of his return to Germany from America, he left for New York once again as a disillusioned exile. The German situation was no longer interesting, it was tragic and demonic. But shortly after arriving in America he found he could not stay away from his country, and so returned, a true patriot and an even more truthful Christian. For him, exile did not mean leaving Germany, but being a stranger and an unwanted alien within Germany. Some South Africans feel like that in the land of their birth: blacks, because they are classified as foreigners, whites, because in their rejection of the racial values and norms of our society they in turn are shunned by the majority of their fellow-citizens. Such blacks and whites seek to be true patriots, but they are declared to be unpatriotic.

But there are those who find they can no longer stay in South Africa. Of course, many blacks have gone into exile and are to be found in every major African, European and North American city; some have joined hands with African forces bent on overthrowing the South African government. There have also been many whites who have left because of political pressure, or because they could no longer stomach the situation. This has been especially true of academics and professional people. It is tempting to leave, and sometimes the decision is not whether to go, but whether to stay. It is also tempting to criticize those who have left without being forced to do so. If only they had remained we would feel stronger! If only they would return, as indeed some have begun to do, we would feel encouraged. Bonhoeffer would have understood why some have left, and why others have stayed, and he probably would have judged neither. He made his own decision to stay in Germany only after the decision to go, and he knew the agony involved in both. He was ruthless with himself, and was only at peace when he knew that he had made the right rather than the expedient decision.

Many South African exiles go because they cannot endure present personal suffering under discriminatory laws; others because, being white, they see no future for themselves and more especially for their children. In the light of this, it is understandable why one of the most persistent questions which South Africans who are concerned about the situation ask each other today is simply: Are changes taking place swiftly enough to give us hope? Perhaps Sir John Lawrence, in his report on a visit to South Africa during 1974, has captured the mood best in his account of a typical conversation:

> I would ask, 'Are there, as some people say, real signs of hope in spite of all?' 'No, everything is getting worse and is certain to get much worse.' And there would follow a catalogue of indisputable facts that it would seem must logically lead to despair. 'So, must one despair?' 'No', and there would follow a recital of precisely the possible points of hope that my first question was designed to elicit. 'But you are contradicting yourself.' 'I know I am. This is South Africa. The facts are contradictory. Some days I despair and some days I hope. In the end I really think that the most rational thing is to hope for a miracle, for a sudden change of heart. There is deep hate here, but there is also deep love.' So many conversations took this shape that I began to look for truth in the contradictions.[5]

Bonhoeffer would have grasped this South African paradox, and discovered the truth in it; indeed, for him ultimate truth was always to be found in the contradiction that God allowed himself to be pushed out of his world on to a cross of shame and degradation. It was precisely this theology of the crucified God which enabled him to interpret reality and discern the signs of the times, and to live in hope.[6] Bonhoeffer was angry with the cynic as well as with those who refused to face reality: 'They think that the meaning of present events is chaos, disorder, and catastrophe; and in resignation or pious escapism they surrender all responsibility for reconstruction and for future generations. It may be that the day of judgement will dawn tomorrow; in that case, we shall gladly stop working for a better future. But not before.'[7] Bonhoeffer wrote this in the Germany of 1943 during 'the race between revolution and arrest'![8]

South Africa dramatically reflects the turmoil and stress of modern society. Hans-Ruedi Weber called it 'the laboratory of the world'.[9] Most of the major problems which face mankind confront us, and the evils of racism are obvious. This laboratory of human relations and power politics has been built on much historical tragedy and contemporary blunder. It is full of shattered dreams, broken resolutions, fear, frustrations, and deep hatred and anger. 'If South Africa can solve her problems,' Dr Weber concluded, 'she will be making a tremendous contribution to the world.' But it does need a few miracles, and these are not cheap to manufacture, in fact, they are the product of costly grace, about which the Church should know something. Moreover, the Church is called to work for a miracle, and therefore to live in anticipation of a miracle. As such it could be a sign of hope.

The struggle of the Church
The Church in South Africa reflects the paradoxical nature of the situation. Indeed, it is difficult even to talk about *the* Church in South Africa because its character and constituency are so diverse and complex.[10] It can be blamed for creating and entrenching apartheid; it can be praised for its prophetic role and its significant part in the creation of articulate black leadership, its ministry of reconciliation, and its sharing in the sufferings of the rejected and despised. But the Church has always been a community both of sinners and saints, so this is nothing new. Bonhoeffer would have added that there is no ideal Church.[11] However, while the Church in South Africa should not overestimate either its own ability or its importance, which means that it should resist the temptation to take itself too seriously, on the other hand, the Church has considerable resources and potential for helping to bring about the kind of changes which the biblical demands of justice and reconciliation require of our land. Is there any word from Bonhoeffer on the subject?

Perhaps he would first refer us to that very powerful section on 'the Confession of Guilt' in his *Ethics* where he writes:

. . . the free confession of guilt is not something which can be done or left undone at will. It is the emergence of the form of Jesus Christ in the Church. Either the Church must willingly undergo this transformation, or else she must cease to be the Church of Christ . . .[12]

The Church in South Africa needs to acknowledge clearly and honestly that it is guilty and responsible for a great deal that is wrong, and that it shares deeply in the total guilt of the nation. Our tendency to justify ourselves before others is beginning to look like an attempt to justify ourselves before God!

> Guilt! I hear a trembling and quaking,
> A murmur, a lament that arises;
> I hear men grow angry in spirit.
> In the wild uproar of innumerable voices
> A silent chorus
> Assails God's ear:
>
> 'Pursued and hunted by men,
> Made defenceless and accused,
> Bearers of unbearable burdens,
> We are yet the accusers.
>
> 'We accuse those who plunged us into sin,
> Who made us share the guilt,
> Who made us the witnesses of injustice,
> In order to despise their accomplices.
>
> 'Our eyes had to see folly,
> In order to bind us in deep guilt . . .'[13]

Bonhoeffer accepted his own solidarity in the guilt of his nation. Too often in South Africa both the nation and the Church fail to recognize their guilt. We are told, and this applies particularly to whites, that a sense of guilt is a sign of weakness, and that it plays into the hands of our country's enemies.[14] How naïve! Of course, a cringing self-flagellation is a sign of weakness, it is an illness, but not so the acknowledgement of guilt when it is real. This acknowledgement is a sign of strength, of moral courage and integrity. It is a prelude to healing, and a means of preventing disaster. The longer we repress our guilt, the longer it will take us to come to terms with our history, to face ourselves and one another without illusion. The repression of guilt only leads to acts of violence and self-destruction. As 'good' South Africans we may not care much about the judgement of others, though I doubt that that is still true, but then our response to their criticisms should not be so paranoiac. In any case, we should be far more fearful of the judgement of God working itself out in our history, and that should give us cause for reflection on any guilt which we may need to acknowledge. But let the Church acknowledge this guilt, let the Church confess the nation's sins, even if the nation refuses to share in the act. For vicarious, representative action is fundamental to the being of the Church.[15]

Bonhoeffer disagreed with Barth's early ecclesiology in which the Church was regarded purely as an act or event. This disagreement is implicit throughout *Sanctorum Communio*, in which Bonhoeffer shows that the Church is not only a means to an end, it is also an end in itself; it is not only an event, but also a community of persons. Indeed, it is nothing less than Christ existing as a community of persons. In spite of the faults in Bonhoeffer's attempt to relate theology and sociology in *Sanctorum Communio*, his intention was correct; it indicated his desire to make and keep ecclesiology concrete. This community of persons exists in the world; it has a structure. And its responsibility is to realize the form of Christ in its concrete existence. This has immediate consequences both for the Church itself and for society:

> The point of departure for Christian ethics is the body of Christ, the form of Christ in the form of the Church, and formation of the Church in conformity with the form of Christ. The concept of formation acquires its significance, indirectly, for all mankind only if what takes place in the Church does in truth take place for all men.[16]

The consequences for the life of the Church should be self-evident. The Church has to put its own house in order. It is no good simply making a 'confession of guilt'. This could so easily become yet another way of escape from concrete reality and obedience. For Bonhoeffer, confession required *metanoia*, radical change or true repentance, which was worked out in the existence of the Church in the life of the world:

> The Church is the Church only when it exists for others. To make a start, it should give away all its property to those in need. The clergy must live solely on the free-will offerings of their congregations, or possibly engage in some secular calling. The Church must share in the secular problems of ordinary human life, not dominating, but helping and serving. It must tell men of every calling what it means to live in Christ, to exist for others. In particular, our own Church will have to take the field against the vices of *hubris*, power-worship, envy, and humbug, as the roots of all evil.[17]

In 1972 the South African Council of Churches and the Christian Institute of Southern Africa published a joint report entitled *Apartheid and the Church*.[18] This report contains some far-reaching concrete proposals for the Church in our land if it is serious in its desire to be the Church of Jesus Christ. The introduction to the section on recommendations reads as follows:

> All too often in the past the Church has regarded recommendations and resolutions as a sufficient response to the needs of men in Church and Society. Such recommendations then have merely a soporific effect on the Church's conscience. A faith which does not issue in action is like a corpse (James 2:26). So the following recommendations, or any mere approval of them, will be of no use without setting up programmes to put them into effect.[19]

Some of the recommendations were already in the process of being implemented before the report was published, and others have since been given serious attention. Moreover, some of the member Churches of the South African Council of Churches have begun to initiate special programmes to deal with the issues, and the Council has initiated its Programme on Justice and Reconciliation to help co-ordinate and support the Churches in their task. At its 1974 National Conference, the Council of Churches also began to consider the Churches' ministry to South African exiles. But no one would be so presumptuous as to think that all is now well! The challenging voice of black theologians makes that abundantly clear:

> It is now time for the black man to evangelize and humanize the white man. The realization of this will not depend on the white man's approval, but solely on the black man's love for the white man. From the black man's side this will mean the retrieval of Christian love from the limitations of the white man's economic and political institutions.[20]

Hopefully, this voice is at last being heard, and the implications of its message have begun to penetrate the life of the Church. There is certainly no room for complacency as the urgency of the task begins to dawn upon us.

But the Church is not only called upon to put its own house in order. For while this search for integrity is essential, the Church does not have to become a model for society before it can speak prophetically to the nation; indeed, there will never be a time when the Church has earned the right to do so on the basis of its own purity. The Church speaks out of a position of shared guilt, not self-righteousness, and while its criticism must always begin within its own life, part of that self-criticism should awaken it to its responsibility to the nation. Bonhoeffer saw this so clearly with regard to the Jewish question. While it was imperative for the Church not to allow race to determine membership, or to affect it in any way, it was also imperative for the Church to protest against racism in society as a whole. The Church could not be content with easing its own conscience, it had a national responsibility. The ecclesiastical issue had immediate political ramifications. This fact is not always clearly seen in our situation, but it is seen nonetheless by a significant number of church leaders and members who recognize that the Church fails to be the *Church* when it is no longer concerned about the righteousness of the nation in the light of the righteousness of God. In other words, the Church is called to be a confessing Church, a Church which confesses the Lordship of Jesus Christ over every aspect of life in society. We cannot think or act as if reality is divided into a sacred and a secular sphere. We dare not sing the Lord's song in our strange land, unless we share the agony of the pained, and participate in the struggle for justice.[21]

In an appendix to this book Eberhard Bethge gives his response to the question 'A Confessing Church in South Africa?' It is probably the kind of response which Bonhoeffer would have given to the same question, and it deserves our serious attention. Ever since the failure of the Cottesloe Consultation in 1960,[22] there has been talk about a confessing Church in South Africa. This discussion reached its peak in 1968 after the publication by the South African Council of Churches of 'The Message to the People of South Africa', which was hailed as an equivalent to the Barmen Declaration.[23] The 'Message' issued in the Study Project on Christianity in an Apartheid Society (Spro-cas), which in turn produced the report *Apartheid and the Church*, with its concrete proposals for the life and witness of the Church. Our situation, like any other, requires that the Church confess Jesus Christ as Lord over against any other ideology, and in so far as the Church does this it is in a state of being a confessing Church. This is absolutely essential, and is the basis of the Church's prophetic role in society. In this regard, the Churches in South Africa have a great deal to learn from the Confessing Church in Germany; they can also learn a great deal from its mistakes, mistakes which Bonhoeffer recognized, and which have been documented and commented upon by others.[24] But it would appear that any attempt to reproduce in South Africa a 'Confessing Church' based on the German model would be based on a misunderstanding of the Church's situation in South Africa, and on a failure to grasp the significant differences between Germany in the 1930s and South Africa in the 1970s.[25] The Japanese theologian

Yoshinoba Kumazawa makes the same point: 'Since the faith is to be confessed in relation to the historical acts of God, confessing the faith must bear an historical character. Specifically it should be *confessio in loco et tempore*: confessing the faith in a certain place and time. We are not going to "repeat" statically what was confessed in the past within a particular situation.'[26] But we must confess concretely that Jesus Christ and not a racial ideology is Lord!

This confession has particular implications for the unity of the Church in South Africa, as Bethge has so rightly indicated in his article. In a land where separation of the races is so fundamental to government policy, the search for church union becomes far more than an ecumenical exercise. It is a struggle for the identity of the Church itself, and therefore, a struggle for its ultimate relevance in the situation. Whatever the merits of black-white polarization may be in the political or economic arenas, it is a contradiction within the Church. This does not rule out the fact that black Christians may have to work together for change in the Church *as black Christians*. What needs to be seen much more clearly is that the search for church union is directly related to justice and reconciliation, and not just to the consolidation of church structures and institutions. Indeed, the movement for church union amongst the Lutheran Churches in South Africa has clearly revealed the true issues facing the Church in our land.[27] The Church Unity Commission, which is working for the union of the Anglican, Congregational, Methodist and Presbyterian Churches, has also realized that its task is directly related to the problems of racism both within and outside the Church itself.[28] There are also promising signs in this regard within the Dutch Reformed Churches. Therefore attempts at church union should not necessarily be interpreted as a means of escape from the realities of the situation.

For a German Lutheran in the 1930s, Bonhoeffer's participation in the ecumenical movement was considerable and significant. Bethge introduces us to this in his chapter on 'True Ecumenism'. Bonhoeffer was basically concerned that the infant ecumenical movement should be founded on good theology, and that it should speak a clear and concrete word to the nations on the pressing issues of the day, which at that historical moment were war and peace. Whether or not he would have agreed with everything that is now associated with the World Council of Churches is open to debate, but his writings and utterances on ecumenism in the mid-1930s leave little room for doubting that he would have applauded the concrete nature of the controversial Programme to Combat Racism. Many Christians in South Africa would agree with him on that point, as indeed the member Churches of the World Council in South Africa have indicated.

What Bonhoeffer would say on the vexed question of implicit support for violence as a means of social change is difficult to say, for even though he shared in the attempt to assassinate Hitler, he only saw that as a last resort.[29] But as the Churches in South Africa increasingly struggle with the question of violence and non-violence, reflection on Bonhoeffer's thought could prove an important source of insight. It is noteworthy that the resolutions accepted by the 1974 National Conference of the South African Council of Churches on the highly controversial subject of conscientious objection provoked indignant white reaction throughout the country. The parallel with Bonhoeffer's position in this regard is quite striking. And this is certainly going to become one of the most agonizing issues to which the Church in South Africa will have to respond. The South African Council of Churches has consistently rejected violence as a means of change and as a means of maintaining an unjust *status quo*.

One of the worst sins in Nazi Germany was to be internationally-minded. Bonhoeffer was surely one of the chief culprits in this regard, for he continually stressed the importance of the ecumenical links between the German Church and the rest of the Christian world. We could well ponder his words afresh:

Under the onslaught of new nationalism, the fact that the Church of Christ does not stop at national and racial boundaries but reaches beyond them, so powerfully attested in the New Testament and in the confessional writings, has been far too easily forgotten and denied. Even where it was found impossible to make a theoretical refutation, voices have never ceased to declare emphatically that of course a conversation with foreign Christians about so-called internal German church matters was unthinkable, and that a judgement or even an open attitude towards these things was impossible and reprehensible.[30]

In the midst of the church struggle, Bonhoeffer's concern took the shape of seeking the recognition of the Confessing Church, as the true Church in Germany, by the ecumenical movement, and of trying to maintain communication and dialogue. Bonhoeffer's correspondence with Geneva makes very interesting reading for those who are familiar with the correspondence between the World Council of Churches and the South African member Churches during the past fifteen years, and especially since the initiation of the Programme to Combat Racism.[31] In his Alden-Tuthill Lectures in Chicago in 1960, Eberhard Bethge correctly anticipated a great deal of what has actually happened, and aroused at least one South African's interest in the subject, when he wrote:

Rouse and Neill's great history of the Ecumenical Movement (1954) does not even mention Bonhoeffer's hot theological discussions with Geneva and with Faith and Order in 1934 and afterward – discussions which would make a good and penetrating textbook for our judgement of the present crisis between the Churches in South Africa and the relation of Geneva to this crisis.[32]

It is absolutely imperative that communication be maintained between the world-wide Christian community and the Church in South Africa, in spite of the tensions between them and the traumatic experiences which the South African Churches have to undergo in our country because of their clinging to this relationship. Although the South African member Churches of the World Council have repeatedly reaffirmed their membership of the World Council, they have also criticized the support for violence implicit in some grants made under the Programme to Combat Racism in Southern Africa. This has meant that on the one hand they have been accused by the State of being unpatriotic and of aiding Communism, and on the other hand they have been accused by many in the ecumenical movement of being racist and supporters of the Government. This is another tension which Bonhoeffer knew from his own experience. The German State regarded him as a traitor, and then, when he worked for the *Abwehr*, many in the ecumenical movement treated him with the gravest suspicion. But Bonhoeffer insisted on the fact that the Confessing Church needed to listen to the voice of the Churches beyond Germany, and that the ecumenical movement for its own sake needed to listen to the voice of the Confessing Church.

In view of the tense relationship between the State and the Churches in South Africa which belong to the World Council and the South African Council of Churches, the question is sometimes asked whether the Churches in South Africa are really free. Writing from New York during his short exile in 1939, Bonhoeffer commented that 'the Americans speak so much about freedom in their sermons. Freedom as a possession is a doubtful thing for a Church; freedom must be won under the compulsion of a necessity. Freedom for the Church comes from the necessity of the Word of God. Otherwise it becomes arbitrariness and ends in a great many new ties. Whether the Church in America is really "free", I doubt.'[33] Christian freedom is a gift of God which is not dependent upon circumstances or the socio-cultural milieu in which the Church finds itself. The Church is therefore not dependent upon the State for its freedom for this is not within the power of the State to grant or withhold. Hopefully there can always be a good working relationship between Church and State, a relationship of mutual trust and interdependence. But this is not what is meant by the freedom of the Church, for real freedom cannot be embodied in a national constitution, it can only be achieved through obedience to the Gospel and righteousness of God. Thus, for Bonhoeffer, there is nothing cheap about freedom; the 'Stations on the Road to Freedom' are discipline, action, suffering and death.[34] Perhaps the Church in South Africa has a unique opportunity to show what Christian freedom really means, as it struggles to be the Church for others.

Theology in context

We have not referred at all in this essay to Bonhoeffer's thinking in prison about Christianity in a 'world come of age'.[35] The reason for this is that his earlier writings appear to be more relevant to our present situation. Moreover, there is a sense in which the Enlightenment as an historical event has passed us by at the southern tip of Africa, and therefore we are still a religious rather than a secular society. Part of the tension between the world-view of the English- and Afrikaans-speaking whites is a result of this historical fact, for the English have been far more deeply affected by secularism. Moreover, part of the tension between white Christianity and black Christianity is also rooted here, for Africa is a religious continent and is highly sceptical of the Western European division of reality into the sacred and the profane. Reality, as for Bonhoeffer, is indeed one, but in Africa it is still generally regarded as religious. Thus, while in Europe and North America the situation may be 'beyond Bonhoeffer' by now, South Africa is largely 'before Bonhoeffer' in these respects.

At the same time, South Africa is a highly industrialized and urbanized country, and it is possible to discern the influence of Bonhoeffer's 'religion in a world come of age' in certain areas of theological reflection in South Africa. This is true in one sense of 'Black Theology', which has become increasingly significant in our country. Whereas 'African Theology' is an attempt to relate Christianity to African culture and spirituality, that is, to religion, 'Black Theology' relates the Gospel to daily reality, and is rooted in the *theologia crucis*. It is a theology of liberation, and as such has gained particular relevance for black urban Christians. In response to the question 'Who is Jesus Christ for us, today?' black theologians answer that he is 'black', by which they mean that he identifies himself with the oppressed and seeks their liberation. 'Black' is therefore not primarily a racial

designation, but a socio-political one. In response to this development, there is now discussion on how those who are not overtly
oppressed may relate in a Christian way to those who are. The
influence of Bonhoeffer is not difficult to discern![36]

The more we reflect on the writings of Dietrich Bonhoeffer, the
more we discover insights which are pertinent to our situation.
For example, what about the relevance of his idea of 'arcane
discipline' in our context? 'Qualified silence might perhaps be
more appropriate for the Church today than talk which is very
unqualified.'[37] We have only attempted, and very inadequately,
to explore some dimensions of his thought with regard to South
Africa. Much more remains to be done. Perhaps *Bonhoeffer:
Exile and Martyr* will provide further stimulation for this task.

Bonhoeffer never visited South Africa, but he did visit North
Africa. If he had visited us, would he have written a similar note
in his diary as he did after his 1924 experience in Libya?

> One should not spend a longer time in Africa without prepara-
> tion, the shock is too great, and increases from day to day, so
> that one is glad to return to Europe again. [38]

Perhaps, he might even have expressed the wish to return to
South Africa. We hope so, not necessarily because we agree with
all his insights and answers, but because we continually need to
hear him ask us the question he always asked himself and those to
whom he spoke: 'Who is Jesus Christ for you in South Africa,
today?'

ONE

Credible Ministry

In 1934 Dietrich Bonhoeffer's father, an eminent psychiatrist and neurologist in Germany, wrote a birthday letter to his son in London:

At the time when you decided to devote yourself to theology I sometimes thought to myself that a quiet, uneventful, minister's life, as I knew it from that of my Swabian uncles and as Mörike describes it, would really almost be a pity for you. So far as uneventfulness is concerned, I was greatly mistaken. That such a crisis should still be possible in the ecclesiastical field seemed to me with my scientific background out of the question.[1]

This quotation shows how firmly the traditional image of the ordained minister was still established at the time when Bonhoeffer decided on his vocation. The role of the minister in society was not really questioned, his identity was clear and his influence was regarded as providing a moral pillar for an authoritarian social order.

The quotation also shows how out of date this profession seemed to the educated person of that time. The father regrets to see his son wasting his excellent gifts of intellect, character and physique on a redundant profession – a servant of religion working outside the heart and core of life.

But there is a third thing we learn from this quotation. Dietrich's father, a typical warm-hearted humanist, enlightened scientist and sceptical empiricist, realizes with surprise that whereas his colleagues, hiding behind scientism as a substitute for religion, had failed so blatantly in the crisis of culture and existence brought about by National Socialism, the Christian ministry had reacted publicly and steadfastly. Furthermore, in doing so, it had responded to its own inner crisis by a renewal of its sense of calling.

Bonhoeffer must have been very happy about this letter. He knew, of course, how sceptical his family had been about the vocation he had chosen. In *Sanctorum Communio* he almost seems to be quoting from the discussions he and his elder brothers and sisters had about professions in their young days when he describes the life of the Church and of the worshipping assemblies of the congregation:

> What purpose is served by the dreary flatness of public congregation, where you risk having to face a narrow-minded preacher alongside spiritless faces?[2]

From the beginning to the end of his life Bonhoeffer lived with the social, institutional and theological crisis of the ministry. He was deeply concerned about its external and internal authenticity, and devoted the gifts of his body, intellect and character in order to grasp the crisis at its core and turn it to positive effect. Seen objectively, this effort, with its different experiments, has sharpened the crisis in the ministry to breaking point. Some people feel he betrayed his calling in the end; others believe he rendered a decisive service to its authenticity.

I. MOTIVATION

Bonhoeffer chose his profession during the First World War when he was still virtually a boy. His cousins were wounded or killed in action. One of his three elder brothers, who all served as soldiers, was killed in 1918, which for many months deeply afflicted his mother, who lived so intensely with and for her children. These events left a deep mark on the sensitive boy and evoked in him a fervent wish to show that a Christian can deal with death. His twin-sister has told us how the youngest children trained themselves, physically and psychically, in thinking of God and nothing else. The boy clearly demanded more of himself and his little sisters than they were able to stand. It remained so throughout his life. Everything he undertook, he did much more seriously than was the custom, or was expected by his teachers. However fond he was of playing, he could not bear playfulness or half-heartedness when it was a matter concerning the ultimate demands on man.

Another motive for his decision may be found in his relation to his brothers and sisters. Not only did he not share his elder brothers' interest in and gift for the sciences, his own interests being more on the literary side, but, as the youngest of the brothers, he had not been able to prove himself, as they had done during the war, and his eager nature found this difficult to bear. So he decided to throw himself into a vocation which demanded the whole person. The stakes could nowhere be higher than in the service of Christ.

When this decision had taken definite form, he was first attracted by the chance it gave him for debate. He was going to expose the scepticism and agnosticism of his elders. With this aim in view, he was going to master the fields of philosophy and theology. Thus he started his studies by concentrating on philosophy, and mainly on the philosophy of the nineteenth century from Kant to Scheler. In a very short time he finished his courses, took his doctorate at the age of twenty-one, and at twenty-four became lecturer at the University of Berlin. His outlook in these years was influenced by the dominant liberal theology in Berlin and then, through reading, by the distant figure of Karl Barth. The former gave him the tools for his thought; the latter, however, directed him, as he himself thought, into the proper and worthwhile workshop.

2. CERTAINTY

However intellectual and academic a course Bonhoeffer's life seemed to take, and however passionately interested in academic theology he remained in later years, we nevertheless discern an opposite tendency at a very early stage, namely, concern for the practical ministry. This much is obvious from the very subject of his thesis, *Sanctorum Communio*. It is the concrete presentness of the Gospel amongst a group of people, in the Church, which interests Bonhoeffer from the beginning, more than any other philosophical and universal implication of the message. His primary concern is not *what* it means, but *where* in fact it can be found.

> The basis of all this is the reality of the *sanctorum communio*, for it is to the *sanctorum communio* that the Word is given, as both creating it and as the instrument of its activity. Where it is present the Word is not ineffective.[3]

Later, too, he emphasized the concreteness of this reality in a way which almost shocked his students:

> We should not allow resentment and dogmatic frivolity to deprive us out of hand of our historical Protestant Church.[4]

He thus indicated that the Church of Berlin, for example, with its councils, consistories and many strange offices, was nevertheless the Church of Jesus Christ. His students found it hard to understand him; a man so critical, and yet apparently obsessed with such a desire for concreteness.

Bonhoeffer had no intention of abandoning academic theological pursuits. Even while involved in parish work as an assistant pastor in Barcelona in 1928 he continued wrestling with current theological problems, and in 1931 published his second major book, entitled *Act and Being*. Nevertheless, again and again we find remarks like the following:

> I feel drawn more and more into the ministry.

> At present I am faced with a pretty momentous decision, whether to take a pastorate at Friedrichshain in East Berlin at Easter. It is strange how hard it is to decide . . . The problem is how to combine the ministry with university teaching.[5]

In spite of his keenness to come to grips with the concrete presentness of the Gospel in the Church and the ministry, Bonhoeffer's interest focused intensely, and at first almost undialectically, on the fact that the certainty of his calling did not depend on himself. The certainty lay beyond the bearer of the message; it was grounded in the transcendent. He was concerned far less about the form the office took, or about the problem of the authenticity of the bearer of the message. Yet for Bonhoeffer this question of authenticity nevertheless involved a deep-seated struggle with himself. He sometimes names his own urge for reflection on the genuineness and authenticity of his motives as his greatest enemy. The question of personal authenticity, when asked of oneself, releases ever new and increasingly vain responses. Hence Luther's insight about the 'heart turned in on itself', and his pointing to the transcendent grounding of his call, meant a real existential liberation for Bonhoeffer and his ministry. Later we shall see that his ever-growing insistence on authenticity retained its significance, but only in conjunction with this deeper insight. Before he realized the importance of personal authenticity for the very sake of the transcendent, he wrote:

> I preach, that is, but I preach in the strength of Christ, in the strength of the faith of the congregation, *not* in the strength of my faith, for, given that during the preaching itself I could overcome temptation in the act of faith, the existential proposition that 'I have been forgiven' would in itself be no vehicle of the ecclesiastical 'thou art forgiven'.[6]

Inasmuch as the Gospel in action is alive, and effective here and now, it lives from 'being' beyond my own realization. So Bonhoeffer, once the identity of his vocation was established as a 'given' derived from a transcendent source, setting aside all questions of personal authenticity, never again questioned it in a way that might have cancelled it from his personal and theological presuppositions. This was especially true at the end of his life when he struggled with the task of the so-called 'non-religious interpretation' of the Gospel. Even then, he never called the validity of his vocation into question.

3. CREDIBILITY

A change took place when, after his ordination, Bonhoeffer began to proclaim the Reformers' Gospel of the transcendent which is 'for us' – *pro nobis*. Emerging from academic debate and research about the relation between the *extra nos* and the *pro nobis*, he now had to share responsibility for its proclamation from the pulpit, and to share in the resolutions of ecumenical church committees, while, at the same time, remaining true to the tradition of the Reformers. Now the certainty of his office, which lay beyond all human realization, called ever more distinctly for authentic representation.

While dealing with these problems, however, Bonhoeffer did not develop a renewed interest in or understanding of the concept of the ministry, as some catholicizing Protestants did! He turned his attention to existence in discipleship which, at the same time, made him more critical of the Church and the ministerial office. This did not mean that he now denied his earlier understanding of the Church as concrete in favour of an invisible Church; on the contrary, he attacked the Church and the ministry in its concrete existence wherever and whenever it betrayed the issues at stake in the world. And he did this for the sake of a more faithful presence in the world.

This change in Bonhoeffer had a personal side to it, but it also found expression in his lecturing, and it brought about a fresh consideration of the Commandments and the Sermon on the Mount. The personal side involved an intensified spiritual discipline. We now hear an occasional remark that he had taken 'rather a dislike' to his theological work, or that he was glad 'to have emerged from the cul-de-sac of so much theology, and returned to these primitive things'.[7] The students in Berlin were surprised that their young teacher began his lectures with prayers, and that he dared to ask direct questions about their piety. Years later, in retrospect, he described this change for the first and only time, in a letter to a woman who at that period shared his thoughts:

I plunged into work in a very unchristian way. An ... ambition that many noticed in me made my life difficult ...

Then something happened, something that has changed and transformed my life to the present day. For the first time I discovered the Bible ... I had often preached, I had seen a great deal of the Church, and talked and preached about it – but I had not yet become a Christian ...

I know that at that time I turned the doctrine of Jesus Christ into something of personal advantage for myself ... I pray to God that that will never happen again. Also I had never prayed, or prayed only very little. For all my abandonment, I was quite pleased with myself. Then the Bible, and in particular the Sermon on the Mount, freed me from that. Since then everything has changed. I have felt this plainly, and so have other people about me. It was a great liberation. It became clear to me that the life of a servant of Jesus Christ must belong to the Church, and step by step it became plainer to me how far that must go.

... The revival of the Church and of the ministry became my supreme concern ...

Later in this letter he went on:

My calling is quite clear to me. What God will make of it I do not know ...

I must follow the path. Perhaps it will not be such a long one. Sometimes we wish that it were so (Philippians 1:23). But it is a fine thing to have realized my calling ...

I believe its nobility will become plain to us only in coming times and events. If only we can hold out.[8]

In his university lectures we now find special reference to the personal confession of sins and the discipline of church members. Parallel to the theological problem of faith and faithfulness is Church and churchmanship – the faithful participation in church life; being open to the Word of God. And there is even reference to Christian devotional exercises, meditation, asceticism, and service. Today all this might be mistaken for escapism. But at the same time Bonhoeffer became interested in pacifism, which was then highly unpopular in Germany, and he was serving his Church in a working-class area of Berlin. He also became involved in the ecumenical movement, which was frowned upon as being internationally-minded. His sermons of that period certainly do not express any retreat into a pietistic ghetto. But he reacted strongly to any sermon of an undisciplined preacher which lost sight of the Gospel it was meant to proclaim.

The way of Bonhoeffer, which led from the academic atmosphere of his home to the university lecturer's desk, and from there to a pulpit in the Berlin of the early thirties, thus forced him to face the question of the authority of the Word that he had to proclaim in terms of its concrete ethical implications. He felt that the transcendence of the usual pronouncements of grace in the sermons of the Reformation Churches lacked concreteness and force: 'I am being tormented by the problem of concreteness in our proclamation.'[9] And he expressed this even more clearly in a despairing letter:

> How is one to preach such things to these people? Who still believes them? The invisibility breaks us to pieces . . . This absurd, perpetual being thrown back on the invisible God – no one can stand it any longer.[10]

Thus Bonhoeffer had his reservations when Barth, by pointing to the eschatological limit of all realization, warned him to beware of keeping his eyes fixed on any realizations in ethics, commandment or obedience. In Barth's censure, that ethics might merely be described as 'demonstrations of' and 'pointers to' and not the thing itself, Bonhoeffer sensed only another chance to escape, and non-obligation justified by a sermon of allegedly pure grace. Bonhoeffer admitted,

> that our Church today cannot utter a concrete commandment. But the question is whether this lies in its essence – its limitation by the ends to which we are moving – or whether it represents decay and loss of substance.[11]

It was because of his anxiety to avoid false authorities that Barth strengthened the eschatological dimension of ecclesiology and ethics. But Bonhoeffer feared any possible escapism. Eschatological prejudice against all concreteness and realization could so elegantly by-pass the Church's real authority and thus prevent it from taking concrete action. Woe to the Church if Barth's warning, which was correct in itself, actually swallowed up the proclamation of the commandments of the concrete Gospel. Thus Bonhoeffer wrote to a friend:

It is now clear to me that Barth himself does not agree with me on this point.[12]

Yet, as he wrote to Barth himself, he did not allow himself to avoid 'these tenacious questions'[13] but impatiently probed ever more deeply into the authority of the preached word. Thus one day he arrived at the Sermon on the Mount, and threw overboard what he had learnt of its Lutheran interpretation:

Do you know, I believe . . . that the whole thing is decisively expressed in the Sermon on the Mount.[14]

At this time *The Cost of Discipleship* was written. This book was about the grace of obedience. In it Bonhoeffer wrote about 'cheap grace', which he believed provided the poison for the self-destruction of the Protestant Church, and 'costly grace', which meant the liberation of man. It is a book which is eminently about the authenticity of the ministry of the Word, and the status of its bearers, that is, it is an ethic for disciples:

Only in the doing of it does the word of Jesus retain its honour, might and power among us . . .
    There is only one other possibility, that of failing to do it. It is impossible to want to do it and yet not do it. To deal with the word of Jesus otherwise than by doing it is to wrong him. It is to deny the Sermon on the Mount and to say No to his word. If we start asking questions, posing problems, and offering interpretations, we are not doing his word.[15]

With specific reference to the ministry, he wrote:

> Since the authorization and equipment of the messengers is absolutely dependent on the word of Jesus, it is essential that nothing should obscure their royal mission or make it incredible.[16]

Bonhoeffer could not possibly answer the crisis of authority with a fresh Catholic concept of ministry, but only with discipleship. For him, that was the worship of the Word Incarnate. Thus he called upon us to suffer with the Word, so that it might remain with us, and we with it.

4. TRAINING FOR MINISTRY

This change in Bonhoeffer proved fruitful when in 1935 he started training ordinands at Finkenwalde.[17] He introduced a style of seminary life entirely novel in the German Protestant tradition. He was successful because his fascinating personality happily coincided with the special situation in church politics. Ordinands were, at that time, ready for any kind of personal commitment if they saw it as a relevant issue for themselves, and one that did not avoid clear decisions in church politics. So far, no other seminary had succeeded in what Bonhoeffer was embarking on, namely, a training in brotherly community and spiritual discipline for future preachers of the Gospel. He carried it through because sacrifice and renunciation were conceived not as ends in themselves but as serving a new freedom, and hence were willingly accepted. Whoever agreed with Bonhoeffer's assertion: 'Only he who cries out for the Jews may sing Gregorian chants', might also adopt the reverse and practise Gregorian chanting! Before the opening of the Finkenwalde courses, he had written:

> The restoration of the Church must surely depend on a new kind of monasticism, having nothing in common with the old but being a life of uncompromising adherence to the Sermon on the Mount in imitation of Christ. I believe the time has come to rally men together for this.[18]

Time for meditation, that is, disciplined daily personal prayer revolving round scriptural texts, a common life and confession, had been proposed by him to his university students as early as 1932, but with little success. Now in 1935 the time seemed ripe for realizing it in connection with work in the seminary, which it would help to stabilize, since all the other conditions of life were bound to remain troubled and improvised. The strongest incentive was Bonhoeffer's own manner of praying within the community, without any manifestation of self. He would give much care and concentration to the preparation of prayers whose language was modelled on that of the Psalms. He repudiated any reproach that he was being legalistic:

It is no good speaking of legalism where the order of our Christian life, the faithful reading of scripture and prayer are concerned. Disorder dissolves and destroys faith; that has to be heard by the theologian who mistakes lack of discipline for evangelical freedom. Whoever is going to take on a full spiritual office without ruining himself and his work in busyness has to learn the spiritual discipline of a servant of Jesus Christ.[19]

The objection of a church leader that 'we haven't the time for meditation now; the ordinands must learn to preach and to catechize', he judged as:

either a total incomprehension of young theologians today, or else a blasphemous ignorance of how preaching and teaching come about.[20]

Thus Bonhoeffer insisted on tightly knitting together the task of preaching with being a preacher, with his style of life and with the authenticity of his existence.

With his great concern for sharing a common life together, Bonhoeffer struck a heavy blow at the traditional understanding of the parochial ministry, which for centuries had retained its peculiarly individualistic character. It speaks highly for Bonhoeffer's reputation that, in these times of struggle, he was able to establish the House of Brethren in which some ordinands formed a team ministry rather than serve individually in parishes of the provincial Churches. In support of his proposal, he adduced the following reasons:

(a) The content and manner of preaching can be sustained with greater objectivity and staunchness by a community than is possible for an individual in isolation. The principal objective, therefore, is not contemplative introversion, but proclamation.

(b) The answer to the now general question as to the nature of the Christian life cannot be given in the abstract, but only by a concrete experiment in communal living and communal awareness of Christ's commandments. Thus the second objective is the theological question of discipleship.

(c) The renunciation of traditional privileges postulates a group of ministers who are always available and who, in a community, will find that concentration which is necessary for service outside. In other words, the church struggle demands a new form of pastoral office.

(d) The community would afford a spiritual refuge to pastors working on their own who, from time to time, would be able to retire there and renew their strength for further service.[21]

When he pressed one of his friends in the church hierarchy to release an ordinand for this purpose, he gave as a reason that the task laid upon him by the Confessing Church implied a new form of pastoral existence. But he went further:

There are two things the brethren have to learn during their short time in the seminary – first, how to lead a communal life in daily and strict obedience to the will of Christ Jesus, in the exercise of the humblest and highest service one Christian brother can perform for another; they must learn to recognize the strength and liberation to be found in brotherly service and communal life in a Christian community. This is something they are going to need.

Secondly they have to learn to serve the truth alone in the

study of the Bible and its interpretation in their sermons and teaching . . .

For this there must be a body of brethren who, without fuss, involve the others in their communal life. That is what the House of Brethren is.[22]

No monastic vows were taken, but the sharing of money, joint decisions, the discipline of confession and prayer, were a matter of course. Two years later the Gestapo put an end to the seminary and the House of Brethren.

The report which Bonhoeffer wrote after the closure, published in the form of a small book entitled *Life Together*, caused a greater sensation than any other of his publications during his lifetime. That the ministry needed reforming was only too obvious; therefore the first attempt at team-work in the name of authenticity was bound to evoke a great interest. But the Finkenwalde experiment was not just an attempt at a structural reorganization of the ministry in the form of a team. It went beyond function. It clarified as well as strengthened the identity of the *office* of the ministry itself. About this time Bonhoeffer prepared a paper on 'making present' New Testament texts. He said:

The decisive freedom in making the kerygma present consists in making it authentic. The real offence to the world in the proclamation of the Church is no longer the intelligibility of its words and texts, cross and resurrection, but its authenticity. Because Church and pastors say this and do that, because the existence of the pastor is the existence of the bourgeois. But the existence of the proclaimer is the medium of the making present. Thus the question in dealing with this subject remains how far by our life and the life of our Church we have already made the Word unauthentic.[23]

5. PREACHER OR PASTOR?

Thus, the long-forgotten distinction between the offices of the parochial minister and the prophetic preacher became prominent again. Once rediscovered, this distinction attacked the image of the parochial minister at its strongest point and hence it was a difficult distinction for Bonhoeffer to make and maintain.

The real situation became clear when the established office of the parish minister, with its financial and legal privileges, proved a serious hindrance to the freedom of proclamation in the Nazi State. Though its social status rapidly declined, the traditional office of the parochial ministry remained, and was nowhere attacked by the state authorities. Clearly, none but a tiny minority would be prepared, under such circumstances, to change the traditional understanding and structure of the ministry.

But Bonhoeffer knew what he was doing when he had tried to join his ordinands together in a community, which, in the case of an emergency, could help them abandon the accustomed support of the parochial office, a manse, an assured income, the right of a seal and all the other 'privileges and duties of the ecclesiastical order'. From 1935 he therefore insisted on the distinction between the offices of the settled pastor and the preacher, a distinction stressed by the Lutherans probably more than by the Reformed Church:

> The preacher's and pastor's office are not identical. The office of the preacher, not of the pastor, is that of the Church. The former is constitutive and remains so. The pastor's office is a special case of the preacher's office. Its form should be adapted to it. The calling of the preacher remains even though we may be scrubbed from the ministry.[24]

It was the parish ministry, with its centuries-old legal basis, which now smothered the authenticity of the preacher's office. This crisis does not seem to have ended in 1945 but appears to have become *the* crisis in the ministry throughout the world. With this distinction between preacher and pastor, Bonhoeffer offered a remedy which clarified and strengthened the theological identity of the ministry even in the midst of its institutional crisis. Thus he carried on an uncompromising fight against the temptation of ordinands to become licensed for the parish ministry of the official semi-state Church. He asked them to accept all financial and legal uncertainties by not allowing the official National-Socialist doctrine any right to tamper with their calling to proclaim the word of God. Sometimes this demand seemed hardly justified when the so-called official *Volkskirche* in 1938 still offered the buildings, the official titles, opportunities of work, the rights of a seal, and a pulpit. Was the illegal preacher expected to bring things to a head by allowing the closing down of buildings, notices of eviction, paying of damages or possibilities of arrest? In those days Bonhoeffer discovered Zinzendorf's comment on Jeremiah 15:19-21, and sent it to all his ordinands:

Do you hear that, you servants of the Lord? You may be suspended, removed, you may lose your income, be turned out of house and home, but you will again become preachers – that is the word of promise! And if you are dismissed from a dozen posts and again get a fresh one, then you are a preacher in thirteen parishes, for in all the previous ones our innocence, our cross and our faith preach more powerfully than if we were there.

And yet the best among his ordinands sometimes asked whether this opposition was not sheer obstinacy. Was that which still existed to be given up? Could the office of preacher exist without the official and legal parochial ministry? Bonhoeffer remained adamant:

The greatest sacrifices now are small compared with what we should lose by wrongly giving in. I do not know anything that is worth our whole-hearted commitment today, unless it is this cause. The main point is, not how many are in it, but that there are at least some.

Do not let us persuade ourselves that over there, in the ranks of the consistories, we should be free to devote ourselves to really basic matters! We should have given up all inward authority there, because we had not remained in the truth.[25]

In this spirit Bonhoeffer encouraged those ordinands who, because they were unfit for military service or had not yet been enlisted, worked every day in factories. Though the Confessing Church hardly recognized the fact, and though its significance was forgotten after the war, these men were in fact 'worker-priests'. He encouraged team-work in contrast to the individualistic parish ministry of one pastor only. Finkenwalde always sent out four-man teams for missionary work. Thus in his seminary he developed missionary groups, because proclamation requires, in content and actual performance, 'brotherly help and fellowship'.

There is the promise of sharing the burden of temptation during preaching in brotherly prayer, confession and forgiveness. This community is necessary so that the nucleus of the local congregation can be summoned to responsibility, by example.[26]

6. THE DESIRE TO PREACH

During the last years of his life in prison, Bonhoeffer did not suffer another crisis about the identity of his calling as is sometimes presumed. The two new elements in his life, firstly, the participation in the political conspiracy against Hitler, which involved non-spiritual activities and sacrifices of integrity and reputation to the limits of what could be endured, and secondly, the 'non-religious interpretation of the Gospel in a world come of age', with their far-reaching consequences, certainly suggest an obvious crisis in the institutional role of the minister. But in reality they contribute to the genuine theological identity of the ministry, by restoring it with terrible but necessary sacrifice. He himself, at any rate, understood these two last elements in his life in this way.

When, in the midst of the conspiracy in 1942, he began to think and plan for the post-Nazi, post-war period, he wrote these words, which are still valid, to those of his students then in the ministry:

We call on you for a new order of your life. For long it has grieved us that everyone wanted to go his own way, separate from his brother. That was not the spirit of Jesus Christ, but of self-will, of laxity and defiance. It has done serious damage to our preaching. No minister today can fulfil his office by himself. He needs the brethren. We call on you faithfully to keep to the daily times for prayer, to meditation on the scriptures and their study. We ask you to claim the help of brotherly discussion and personal confession, and we charge you with the holy duty of being at your brother's disposal for this service. We ask you to come together, in prayer, when preparing a sermon and to help one another to find the proper words.[27]

In Tegel prison he expressed the desire to become a preacher but not a parish minister again, when the present strife was over. Then the insights of these shocking times of unauthenticity would have to be gathered in. Then there must be service, listening, and even silence. What Bonhoeffer indicated with his words about the 'secret discipline' belongs here too.[28] When in 1944 I faced the possibility of serving as a chaplain in the German army in Italy, and I let him know that the difficulty of having to preach in these circumstances might be too much to bear, he wrote:

One has to live for some time in a community to understand how Christ is 'formed' in it (Galatians 4:19); and that is especially true of the kind of community that you would have.[29]

This 'living for some time' meant, not being talkative, but first living with one another in solidarity and waiting for the hour when the questions are asked, that is, for the hour of authenticity. It was like that for Bonhoeffer even at Tegel. On the last day of his life in Schönberg, he preached only after being asked to do so by everybody, including an atheist, Molotov's nephew.

Bonhoeffer's understanding of his calling does not create any crisis of faith in the role and identity of the preacher, but it does call into question the traditional patterns of the parochial ministry on the grounds of credibility. Bonhoeffer sincerely wanted to preach the Gospel of God's grace for us, but he could not imagine himself in any secure parish situation. Either this insight has been forgotten in Germany today, or else Bonhoeffer was just naïve about the future!

TWO

A Church of Integrity

Dietrich Bonhoeffer and Paul Tillich were alike in many ways, but different in others. Paul Tillich commented on this in a conversation I had with him in 1961. Tillich grew up in the manse of a Prussian village in Brandenburg, a hundred kilometres east of the Berlin metropolis. For his young mind it was a great discovery to find that there was a world beyond the Church, that there were such things as philosophy and socialism. In a sense, the Church lay behind him, and the world ahead. Bonhoeffer, however, grew up in the great city, in the atmosphere of modern science, and amidst the culture of the educated middle class of Berlin. For him it was a discovery to find the Church, with its fascinating history of theology. Thus in Tillich we find tendencies to secure a place for religion in his newly discovered world, and to prove it was still necessary. He renewed apologetics. Bonhoeffer, on the other hand, started off as a conqueror and, though certainly as critical as Tillich, never became an apologist on behalf of the Church. Tillich was interested in the questions of meaning and man's view of the world. He became a professor and remained one. He was never too committed to the Church, whereas Bonhoeffer was anxious to leave the lecturer's desk for the pulpit, trying to separate the questions about religion from the task and life of the Church. He committed himself to the Church, this group of people, their actions, their guilt and their vision. He became one of their ministers.

Having discovered the Church, Bonhoeffer took her more seriously than she was accustomed to being taken, and never ceased to appeal for more appropriate forms of life and witness to replace perverted ones.

There is a word that when a Catholic hears it kindles all his feelings of love . . .

And there is a word that to Protestants has the sound of something infinitely commonplace . . . indifferent and super-fluous . . . – and yet our fate is sealed if we are unable again to attach a new, or perhaps a very old meaning to it . . .

Yes, the word to which I am referring is 'Church' . . .[1]

This is what he said in a sermon in Barcelona in 1928. The Universal Church was the discovery of the young traveller to Rome in 1923. It became the subject of his own first theological work, *Sanctorum Communio*.

I. CHRIST AND THE CHURCH

In *Sanctorum Communio* Bonhoeffer laid the basis for his ecclesiology. He never retracted any of its most important points, although there were developments, and the stresses shifted. There were, for example, such reorientations as the changing of 'all men for the Church' at the beginning to 'the Church for all men' at the end; that is, from a triumphant Church to a servant Church. Ernst Lange calls it a move from an ontological ecclesiology in *Sanctorum Communio* to a purely functional one in the *Letters and Papers from Prison*.

Bonhoeffer's basic concern, however, remained: 'Christ existing as community.' This ecclesiology welded together theological and sociological categories. It indicated that the Church can never be traced back to human need, to some religious *a priori* or meaning in man, or to his instinct for sociality. It can only be traced back to Christology. And Christology cannot be complete without an ecclesiology.

In Bonhoeffer's own history each of these two dimensions interacted again and again, thus providing fresh concepts and leading to new depths of understanding. There were times, notably at the end of his life, when Christology had pride of place in Bonhoeffer's thought. Its critical function seemed over-whelmingly powerful beside all ecclesiological realities. There were other times when ecclesiology came to the fore and seemed to represent a legitimate Christology almost exclusively. This was so at the beginning, at the time of *The Cost of Discipleship*, and during the church struggle.

By thus founding ecclesiology on Christology, Bonhoeffer did not allow his criticism of the Church to lapse into despairing laments and negativism. It made his criticism hard and aggressive, but also rich in vision, decision and action. The fundamental interrelation between ecclesiology and Christology also protected the latter from abstractness. Bonhoeffer never thought of Christ as existing without the social group which belongs to him – whether this group was, as at first, the empirical Christian community, or whether, as at the end, it embraced a limitless, unbounded community beyond it.

When Bonhoeffer started lecturing in Berlin he gave two main series of lectures. One series, on 'The Nature of the Church', was given in the summer of 1932, and the other, on 'Christology', a year later. This order of his lectures represents a theological programme which indicates that even before Barth did so, Bonhoeffer studied theology only within, and on the basis of, the witness of the Church. Though we again have our doubts about it now, at that time it sounded very revolutionary and novel for the Protestant Church when Bonhoeffer said: 'The empirical Church is the presupposition and subject of theology.'[2]

The title of the lectures, 'The Nature of the Church', was probably formulated with a polemical nuance. They were delivered in the very place where, twenty-five years before, Adolf von Harnack had given his famous lectures on 'The Nature of Christianity', afterwards to become a best-selling book. The title chosen was also, perhaps, a polemical reminder of Feuerbach's decisive work of 1841, *The Essence of Christianity*. Bonhoeffer now lectured on the essence of the *Church*. For subsequent generations such a title may smack a little of that triumphalism which Barth anathematized in Otto Dibelius' famous book, *The Century of the Church*. But Bonhoeffer did not mean it that way. He immediately distanced himself from such a triumphalism by speaking of the 'place of the Church' as empirically realizable at the Cross. He sharply contrasted the position sought after by the Church herself, and the position ordained for her by God. In the year before the great church storm broke in Nazi Germany he spoke as we may speak of the Church again today:

> On the one hand the Church today is characterized by having no fixed place and address. She adapts herself, wants to be everywhere, cannot be grasped and hence cannot be attacked; she is on the run from herself, disguised – she became the world, but the world did not become Church. Her existence is that of the fleeing Cain. Sects are being taken more seriously, because they can be located.
>
> . . . On the other hand, in losing her authentic place, she can be found at privileged places of the world only, forfeiting her sense of place. Now she is being hated for occupying her privileged places in the middle class and in conservatism. Her service only meets the needs of the petty bourgeois, not those of the business leaders, of the intellectuals, the godless and revolutionaries. She has settled down in the ceremonies of the world.
>
> Her new independent place since 1918 (O. Dibelius) is not the place befitting her, but the place apportioned to her as a donation by the autonomous civilization. Which is her authentic place? God's will chooses it. [3]

The authentic place of the Church is assigned by Christ the vicarious Representative. He gives the Church her shape and her place, and she retains this form and place through the preaching of redemption, which enables her to become a Representative.

The first confession before the face of the world is the action which interprets itself. If the action becomes a power, the world will ask for the confession of the word too.[4]

We may note this quotation especially in view of Bonhoeffer's later remarks about the Church while he was in prison. Bonhoeffer expressly repudiates perfectionism and prefers to speak about the Church of forgiveness. For him, she is, and remains part of the world.

> Her real worldliness is that she can renounce everything except Christ and the forgiveness of sins . . . The kingdom of God is being revealed, not brought in by force.[5]

This ecclesiology provided a strong base during the following years and proved an impregnable fortress against the National-Socialist heresy. But the fortress was rather closed in on itself. In the lecture of 1932, in the section which bears the promising subtitle 'The Acting Community', there is no mention of what we would expect today of the Church in the field of social ethics; instead, we have: proclamation, assembly, creed. There is something about the structure of the congregation, about being with and for one another, about sacrifice, intercession, confession and pastoral service. There are marginal notes here and there, of a humanistic, revolutionary tenor, but they are not developed. But sentences serving the Church's own ends, like the following: 'The intercession for all men draws them into the community', qualify this dimension.[6] This closedness was a strength, but also a weakness and a danger to which the Confessing Church eventually succumbed, despite her nonconformism as developed by Barth and Bonhoeffer.

2. THE CHURCH AND RACE

After reading my biography of Bonhoeffer, Barth wrote to me in May 1967:

> It was new to me above all else that Bonhoeffer was the first, yes indeed almost the only theologian who in the years after 1933 concentrated energetically on the question of the Jews and dealt with it equally energetically. For a long time now I have considered myself guilty of not having raised it with equal emphasis during the church struggle (for example in the two Barmen Declarations I composed in 1934). But then such a text

would not have been acceptable either to the Reformed or the General Synod, given the spiritual predisposition of even the 'Confessing Christians' in 1934. But this does not excuse the fact that I (my interests lay elsewhere) did not offer at least formal resistance in this matter at that time.[7]

Bonhoeffer, notwithstanding his rather closed ecclesiology, became alert, and irksome to his own Church, as early as 1933, on two questions: the Jewish problem and peace. The Confessing Church was dominated by a concern for confessing 'Christ alone', and the problems of anti-Semitism and peace remained marginal for a long time. But Bonhoeffer related the humanist element in the Jewish question to the confessional question at a remarkably early date.

An interesting illustration of this is his essay 'The Church and the Jewish Question', written in April 1933.[8] It was provoked by the new law 'For the Reconstruction of the Civil Service' of 7 April 1933. This placed a certain group of people on a separate legal basis on racial grounds, making them second-class citizens for purely biological reasons. It is an interesting essay because it mixes conservative Lutheran with progressive revolutionary elements. It was a paper read to a group of Berlin ministers at a time when hardly anybody in the Church was prepared to touch the subject; in fact one member objected to it and another left the meeting. The consequences of the treatment of the Jews by the State were brought home to Bonhoeffer very early through the case of his brother-in-law; of their treatment by the Church through the case of his friend, Pastor Franz Hildebrandt. He immediately realized that the authenticity of the Church was at stake at this point. Very few others recognized this. But the future of Christianity was in the balance.

The Church is in great trouble with the Jewish question, which has caused the most sensible people to lose their heads and forget their Bible.[9]

In Bonhoeffer's opinion the Church was now called upon to

make her position clear in two directions: first, by defining her attitude to the actions of the State and those victimized by it; and second, by considering how the position of baptized Jews affected her in her community life and structural forms, if the separate legal rights of the Jews were applied to the Church. The second subject later became dominant and was the only one dealt with by the Confessing Church. In his paper, Bonhoeffer deals with it under point two. His passionate concern is still the whole problem, especially the first issue concerning the place of the Jews in the nation itself. We are struck by the pains he takes not to allow any liberal humanism to motivate and direct his argument. He begins by saying:

> Both questions can only be answered in the light of a true concept of the Church.[10]

The basis of these answers describing the relation between State and Church seems outmoded today. In the 1932 lectures on the Church the State was seen according to Lutheran tradition as God's other great supporter of order, and thus furnished with the highest dignity. It was the second God-given frontier within the world, next to the kingdom of God. This frontier may be struggled against, and sometimes broken, but only in order to reaffirm it again. In the German tradition the State had pride of place before society, and even the Weimar Republic was increasingly concerned to make democracy into the State, and not the State into a democracy. Bonhoeffer, likewise, in his essay on the Jewish question does not show any passion for democracy and liberalism but states the almost mystically elevated right of the State not to have 'its specifically political actions tampered with' by the Church, and expressly includes the problem of the Jews in Germany. Thus Bonhoeffer remained within the framework of Lutheran ecclesiology and the political science of his time, and none of those present took umbrage on this issue.

They noticed, however, that there were some unusual, heavily weighted, marginal asides, as for instance, that it was a matter for the humanitarian societies and some individual Christian men, among whom he probably counted himself and his family, who felt it was their duty, to remind the State of the moral aspect of its measures – that is, to accuse the State of offending against morality, should the occasion arise. Moreover, a strong State needs such associations and individuals and will foster them by a certain amount of reserved encouragement.[11] There is no mention, as yet, that in this regard not only individual Christians but also the Church might have tasks to fulfil. Bonhoeffer probably had to begin in so conservative and Lutheran a way in order to be heard at all. But even with this Lutheran dressing he was not heard. For unlike practically every churchman of that time, including Martin Niemöller and Hans Lilje, he not only did not speak approvingly of the renewal of the State in 1933, he also went in a new ecclesiological direction. He no longer argued in favour of the static self-preservation of the Church, but emphatically in favour of her action. Certainly, his answers in the paper became more far-reaching than his anti-humanistic motivation.

Bonhoeffer envisaged three areas where action by the Church would become necessary. Firstly, the Church must ask the State 'whether it could answer for its action as legitimate state action . . . In relation to the Jewish question, the Church must now put that question with the utmost clarity.' Except for the memorandum of 1936, even the Confessing Church had never really put that question 'with clarity'. Secondly, under all circumstances the Church will have to care for the victims of state actions, 'even if those victims do not belong to the Christian community'. This was something that needed to be said! In April 1933 Bonhoeffer regarded these two points not merely as possibilities of a far-away future. 'In the Jewish question the first two possibilities for the Church today will be the exigencies of the hour.' We hardly understand today why Bonhoeffer, who saw everything so clearly, remained aloof from all humanitarian motivation and help.

And thirdly, Bonhoeffer envisaged the most radical action. The possibility 'not only of binding up the victims beneath the wheel but also of putting a spoke in that wheel'. At that time he thought of such revolutionary action, whereby the State would be attacked directly by the Church, as only a future possibility which he hoped would not have to be realized. All the same, he anticipated it as early as April 1933. The responsibility for it would, so he hoped, be taken on by an ecumenical council. Such a council never came into existence; the Church failed him and hardly adopted a clear attitude on the first two points at issue. One day Bonhoeffer would have to act out his convictions in lonely decision, when the Church remained silent in the face of the 'Crystal Night',[12] and of Auschwitz. He would feel himself driven into the conspiracy.

This essay marks a certain break in Bonhoeffer's life. Traits of Lutheran institutional absolutism still linger, but they have actually become suspect. The problem of the authenticity of the Church in an increasingly threatening situation changed Bonhoeffer's way of speaking about the Church, made it more critical of her privileges and grounded it afresh in Christology. He now expected to assume responsibilities in the political and humanitarian field.

3. THE CHURCH AND THE STATE

Although Bonhoeffer opposed legal discrimination against the Jews, he did not as yet do so on behalf of what we now call human rights. In the spring of 1933 almost nobody in the Church publicly criticized the abolition of all human rights and freedoms (abolition of the freedom of speech, the press, public assembly, parliamentary controls, the privacy of post, telegraph and telephone; the identification of opposition to the government with hostility to the nation – in short, all the laws of March 1933). Instead, churchmen applauded the establishment of order, the rescue of the nation from the liberalistic-democratic decay, protection against the threat of Bolshevism, the putting into effect of the Lutheran doctrine of the orders of creation, and the abolition of the consequences of the Versailles Treaty. Friedrich Gogarten wrote in 1933: 'When a nation like ours has to be brought back to the form it had lost, it has first to be put into uniform.'[13]

It was only when the Church herself was confronted by the State, through the imposition of a *Reichsbischof* and the implementation of the racial laws in its own life, that there was an upsurge of concerted opposition. Out of this opposition came the now famous Barmen Declaration,[14] which is unparalleled in the history of modern Protestantism. Bonhoeffer welcomed it with relief and fought for its unqualified acceptance to the end. It was a confession in which Christology and ecclesiology were combined; confessing to the one and only revelation of the Word of God in Jesus Christ, and rejecting all other props for this Word; confessing the Church as the People of God on earth with visible structures, precisely because it belonged to Christ. Barmen introduced into German Protestant theology an almost euphoric ecclesiological self-consciousness such as had not existed for centuries, and as Bonhoeffer himself had not even felt it in 1932, when his concept of the Church was so critical. In 1932 there existed an unopposed established Church, but by 1934 the position had radically changed. Now that the Church found herself in a state of crisis, the ecclesiology of Barmen, with which Bonhoeffer identified himself, stressed the gifts of the Church with far more confidence than it did her claims.

However, after Barmen the Confessing Church attached the greatest importance to seeing and interpreting the church struggle as a purely *church* affair. On no account was it to be regarded as a political, humanist or even an ideological struggle. At the beginning Bonhoeffer sympathized with this interpretation, especially in the ecumenical field. Yet after the Confessional synods he kept asking, anxiously, for a word on behalf of the Jews and of peace, especially after the Synod of Steglitz in 1935, which followed the Nuremberg Party Rally at which laws had been proclaimed for wholesale discrimination against the Jews. But he too would have considered it a weakening, if not a betrayal of the issue, if the synods of Barmen and Dahlem had struck political and humanist notes.

To be sure, the real danger of ecclesiastical narrowness at that time was not great. The continual affirmation of the '*solus*

Christus' brought so much liberation in the human realm, amidst
the cries of '*solus* Adolf Hitler', that nobody would have dreamt of
saying that a separate church ghetto was being built. On the
contrary, confessing the '*solus*' created breathing-space and
effected a liberating nonconformism. Long-severed relations, like
the ones between conservatives and liberals, agnostics and
believers, artists and politicians, were healed, for all seemed to
grasp again why there was a Christian community and the worship of God, and what confession of Christ might mean. After
Barmen there existed a fighting faith relevant to the times, which
prevented introverted speculations, just as in Bonhoeffer's *Cost of
Discipleship* the exclusive interest in a Christ-related ecclesiology
was actually identical with the human experience of freedom.
When in later years this identity became blurred, Bonhoeffer
spoke about Barmen as Law and Barmen as Gospel in order to
reveal this identity afresh.

The difficulties of interpreting Barmen increased when the
State directly intervened in order to destroy the Confessing movement by direct laws and orders for church affairs. This was always
done in the guise of the State being a good broker on behalf of
the muddled, fighting churchmen! In other words, the attack
was no longer through Nazi Christians in the Church, who, until
now, had been fought 'unpolitically' as heretics. Now a new
situation arose for the Confessing Church, one which had been
foreseen by Bonhoeffer in his earlier paper on the Jews: the
Church had not only to maintain a space for nonconformism
within herself, but to oppose state legislation and, after 1935, even
demand such opposition from the pulpit. Ecclesiology and church
history had not prepared them for this, and men like Bonhoeffer
stood out more and more in loneliness.

At the same time the realm in which the fight for the very
existence of the Church was being carried on narrowed down.
One defeat followed another, and from 1938 people no longer
felt free to point to the blatant injustice done to men, like that
of the infamous 'Crystal Night'. The silence about humanity was
concomitant with a stiffening of orthodoxy, and the loss of the

real spirit of Barmen through quoting it again and again. True, the self-understanding of the church struggle as being a pure church struggle hardened once again, but what had once been strength now turned into weakness. And when Hitler started his aggressive war, the Confessing Church gave no help, no guidance, no directive to its perplexed members. Barth wrote in 1938-9:

> Many of the best people in the Confessing Church still close their eyes to the insight that the Jewish question, and beyond that the political question as such and as a whole, has become a question of faith today.[15]

At the outbreak of war, ministers of the Confessing Church volunteered, for whatever motives, for active service. It is strange to record the fact that in the end almost two thousand ordained ministers of the Protestant Church were killed in action in Hitler's war, if not for it, and only twenty men serving the Church were killed for the sake of the Gospel. And this helps to explain Bonhoeffer's way into the conspiracy, as well as his ecclesiological change. The Confessing Church had

> lapsed . . . into conservative restoration. The important thing about that Church is that it carries on the great concepts of Christian theology; but it seems as if doing this is gradually just about exhausting it.[16]

4. THE BEING AND FUNCTION OF THE CHURCH

In Bonhoeffer's next phase too, during which he wrote his *Ethics*, his ecclesiology retained its basic presupposition, namely that 'Church' means the relation of Christ to the world. But now the Church no longer figures with only the State as the other of the two exclusive divine bearers of this relation. His understanding of the doctrine of the two kingdoms was changing. In the *Ethics* the Church became one of at least four holders of the mandates through which God is witnessed and served. None of these mandates dominates the others, nor can any of them exclusively claim and possess man. The mandates, which are held by Church, family, labour and government, are adjusted ' "with", "for" and "against" one another', and there is no 'absolute authority of the mandate of the Church'.[17] The mandate of the Church is proclamation. 'True worldly living . . . is possible and real only "in, with and under" the proclamation of Christ.'[18] This is reminiscent of Bonhoeffer's very first writings, but now it becomes the central theme, namely 'that a genuine worldliness is possible solely and exclusively on the basis of the proclamation of the cross of Jesus Christ'.[19] In other words, the Church must serve to set worldliness free.

In fulfilling this mandate of proclaiming true worldliness, the function of the Church is still seen by Bonhoeffer, at this time, in terms of the community by itself. Bonhoeffer's later development of a more functional concept of the Church (as it has been called) is not in evidence here. This important fact is frequently overlooked today. For Bonhoeffer, proclamation can never be reduced to a function, for it arises out of being. The Church *is* part of mankind as accepted by God in Christ. Thus, there will always be the tension, there has to be, between being and function, just as only he can truly fulfil a task who has an identity of his own. And this again depends on the identity of being received in faith from Christ. Thus for Bonhoeffer, even at this stage, the Church does not empty herself in the fulfilment of her task. There remains the tension that

the proclamation of the lordship of Christ over the whole world must always be distinguished from the 'law' of the Church as a community, while on the other hand the Church as a community is not to be separated from the office of proclamation . . .

The Church as a self-contained community is subject to a two-fold divine ordinance and rule. She must be adapted to the purpose of the world, and precisely in this she must be adapted to her own purpose as the place at which Jesus Christ is present.

The peculiar character of the Church as a self-contained community lies in the fact that in the very limitation of her spiritual life and material domain she gives expression to the unlimited scope of the message of Christ, and that it is precisely this unlimited scope of the message of Christ which in its turn is a summons into the limited domain of the congregation.[20]

Here, Bonhoeffer tried to distinguish between being and function while at the same time seeing them closely knit together. Even now he spoke of the Church 'existing for her own ends', and of her task of being the means to an end. Doubtless the Church's function had by now assumed an interest different from that which it had had in 1932, and in *Sanctorum Communio*. Being seems to have entered function, and yet they are not the same. Bonhoeffer was never interested merely in what had to be achieved, and how it was to be done, but rather in *who* did it, what the situation was like, and the relation between the proclaimer and the hearer.

This basic concern did not change during his imprisonment either, though his personal way of proclamation differed then from the normal Sunday morning sermon. He had meanwhile identified himself with the conspirators to an extent which almost completely drove him as a preacher into becoming incognito. Moreover, the preaching Church was fast losing face; Auschwitz had happened, and communication was severely hampered for the usual evangelizing approach. So in trying to be authentic the preacher could assume a disguise, become silent, and risk being misunderstood.

In fact, the letters from prison contain phrases that have been interpreted as if Bonhoeffer affirmed the end of the Church. I myself thought so at the time, with some anxiety! In a letter of 3 June 1944, I asked him: 'How is the abandonment of all room for the Church to be avoided?' I feared a shrinking, a blurring of Church and world, and presumed a total change into mere function was at hand. Only gradually did we grasp how Bonhoeffer's thrust was aimed at a church tradition which was preserved even by the Confessing Church. He attacked not only certain structures of thought, but also the whole Church, with its established privileges and partial character, and its firmly entrenched structures of guardianship and paternalism over man which had to be exposed, and perhaps changed. In this context we understand his ecclesiological words from the prison letters: 'The Church is the Church only when it exists for others.'[21] Even so, Bonhoeffer's thinking and speaking must not be deprived of their dialectical tensions, as if the being and function of the Church had now become one for him.

We have to remember that Bonhoeffer never ceased being truly attached to his Church, and that to many modern readers the prison letters must indeed appear pious. These letters speak quite positively about worship and liturgy, though Bonhoeffer's thought ran in the main along different lines. He promised to ponder over questions of worship later, but he did not live to do so. Ernst Lange now wonders 'whether this could have happened at all' as, in Tegel prison, Bonhoeffer's attitude veered round by 180 degrees. Once he had said: 'The being-for-others of the Church is decided by her being Church.' But now he could say: 'The being Church of the Church is decided by her being for the world.'[22] But even in prison Bonhoeffer did not empty the Church's being into her doing. A famous passage from the baptism letter says that what remains for the Church to do will be confined to praying for and doing right by our fellowmen. And the sentence which deals with solidarity with the world, at the same time asks about the proprium of being a Christian: 'In what way are we "religionless-secular" Christians, in what way are we the *ecclesia*, those who are called forth, not regarding ourselves from a religious point of view as specially favoured, but rather as belonging wholly to the world?'[23] He not only asked: 'In what way are we solidarizers?' but also: 'In what way are we, in solidarity, truly Christians?' Thus being Church is decided by being for the world. But that which is *also* decided is its *being* Church. Act and Being can hardly be separated, but neither are they the same. Being is not dissolved in function, and the tension between solidarity and distance is not removed in favour of the former.

But something else happened. The tradition of demonstration and authoritative and public speech in the Church's preaching and evangelizing was withdrawn into a kind of secret place, an arcane discipline. This had always been in Bonhoeffer's mind when he spoke of a qualified silence of the Church for the sake of her speaking with greater authority later on; that is, the time would have to be awaited when the costly would no longer be wasted irrelevantly, and sold cheaply. Therefore in Tegel prison, too, the 'prayer and righteous action',[24] was stressed in order to avoid the ineradicable misunderstanding that the proclamation of Christ meant a clerical tutelage and religious claim in disguise.

Of course, it is difficult to work such a state of affairs into the routine of our present church practice, with its Sunday sermons and missionary offices, and patterns of mandate conceived as prophetic. Still, even today there are certain forms of life within the Church that embody it, like some of our modern communities. Even work in a parish office looks different when an authoritarian evangelizing is abandoned, and questions are raised about relevance and reality. Thus, the points at issue, and relations to partners, will shift with time.

Until his death, Bonhoeffer always knew and recognized a true caring for the identity of the Church, for her being. He expected a real concern for this identity, which exists in and through Christ, through whom, in turn, a legitimate approach to this identity is possible in listening, asking, praying, exhorting, comforting, sharing, accepting one another. But this identity cannot be demonstrated. Only a weak identity exhibits itself. A strong one is capable of bearing the incognito of 'participation in the powerlessness of God in the world'.[25]

A danger would be to care for the Church's identity in a way which leads to a clerical narcissism. Hence we must say: 'The Church is her true self *only* when she exists for others.' Without an identification with others to the limit of self-surrender, the identity dies. The Church has to identify herself with the world in which she lives. It is the fear of identity – one of the basic fears of man – which makes him stick to the old structures. For the German Church this means sticking to the parish structure, while other Churches have long existed in the framework of voluntary assemblies, or even as dispersed Christian groups. Whenever new identifications are not made, the identity wastes away, the Church loses her face, does not count, becomes boring, has only a few very queer identities instead of the surprising ones which provoke the world to ask questions. But in the presence of Christ both are given to the Church: her identity, and the freedom of identifying herself with her world.

THREE

True Ecumenism

In 1925 the 'Life and Work' movement was constituted in Stockholm. In Germany there was not much sympathetic publicity. Influential groups in the Churches shared the view of nationalist-minded Germans that even the ecumenical movement would not help to remove the discrimination against Germany based on the Versailles Treaty. However, the foremost representatives of ecclesiastical Berlin, and the champions of the unity of the Church in the theological faculty at Berlin University, became committee members of this organization of the future.

In the same summer nineteen-year-old Dietrich Bonhoeffer was a student in this ecumenically progressive faculty. Among his papers dating from those months is a letter from a fellow-student which, though not dictated by any nationalistic resentment, speaks with youthful contempt:

> The more one has to do with it, the more dubious it seems; it would not be dubious if its aim was to be no more than an international meeting for the cultivation of ethics – but the aim is to be much more than that. It is to build the kingdom of God.[1]

The same year Bonhoeffer chose the subject of his doctoral thesis, *Sanctorum Communio*, proleptically passing in it all the strictures of an impatient young man on this new universalist enterprise of Stockholm which, dominated by Anglo-Saxons, was proceeding in a humanist and pragmatic manner. At the same time his attachment to his new idol, Karl Barth, began. Barth, as we know, was only willing to be a member of one of the committees of the embryonic World Council in 1932.

By 1932, however, Bonhoeffer had become quite committed to the ecumenical movement, and, strangely enough, to that organization which theologically was the most dubious, and certainly the most philanthropic and humanistic of them all: The World Alliance for Promoting International Friendship through the Churches. In 1933 ecumenism practically became a creed for Bonhoeffer. Today we regard him as one of the great champions of the ecumenical movement, perhaps the greatest ecumenical figure in German Protestantism, even though his actions and his posthumous work for the ecumenical movement are only fragmentary. Visser 't Hooft wrote:

> When we heard of his death we said to each other what a profound tragedy it was that Bonhoeffer was taken from us before he had any opportunity to make his personal contribution to the ecumenical movement. We were wrong. He has made that contribution all the same.[2]

The history of Bonhoeffer's connection with the ecumenical movement is fascinating because it is full of tensions. With all his cosmopolitan disposition, cultivated by education and the gift of languages, and all his curiosity about everything unknown, he first shut himself off from the Stockholm movement by sharply concentrating on a theology of the Church which excluded any really concrete ecumenism. Then he opened himself to that movement whose entire pragmatic aim was to work for peace, making life difficult for himself by his demand that, there of all places, a theology of ecumenism should be developed. When the ecumenical movement, assisted by its German members, devoted itself more intensely to theological discussion, he accused it of escapism, saying that not theological discussion, but ecclesiastical decision was what was to be expected from its earlier humanism. And when at last, in 1939, the ecumenical movement could have saved him, he turned his back on it. Paradoxically, it is his final entrance into German particularism which has made him ecumenically so alive and effective today.

I. MOVEMENT OR CHURCH?

Bonhoeffer was dragged into ecumenical responsibility, he did not go of his own will. His ecclesiastical chief in Berlin, Superintendent Diestel, an ecumenical veteran himself, can boast of having won Bonhoeffer over. In a birthday letter to the old gentleman in November 1942 Bonhoeffer himself describes what happened:

> It may have been just one phone call in December 1927 – which directed my life into a channel which it has never since left nor, indeed, will ever leave. At that time you asked me ... whether I was willing to go to Barcelona as a probationer. A few weeks later my first meeting took place with a German-speaking congregation in a foreign land and with ecumenical Christianity.

This meeting in Barcelona, however, did not as yet have any great effect.

> There was another phone call in May 1930. You offered me the fellowship at Union Theological Seminary for 1930 to 1931 ... which ever since has been of the greatest importance to me.

But still Bonhoeffer was not at all interested in the ecumenical organizations.

> I was hardly back when you invited me – and this was perhaps the most decisive event – to accompany you to Cambridge.

In Cambridge the great conference of the World Alliance took place in 1931, and the young Bonhoeffer was immediately nominated as one of its youth secretaries:

> For you, these were quite secondary things beside the amount of work you were involved in; but for me, they became a basis for my whole thought and life.[3]

What happened by accident, and not very logically, developed in fact into the most momentous decision of his life. It furnished Bonhoeffer with those connections and experiences which later led him into the conspiracy and finally to Tegel prison.

Of the world ecumenical organizations the World Alliance for Promoting International Friendship through the Churches was the one where you would least expect to find a strict German Barthian theologian. The World Student Christian Federation was the most intellectual group, the International Missionary Council the most evangelical, 'Life and Work' the most clerical, and 'Faith and Order' the most theological. To 'Faith and Order' belonged the theological cream of the great Churches; but Bonhoeffer never entered into a lasting working relationship with it. A platform serving for the discussion of the development of theological understanding between the Churches was too non-committal for him. In fact, during the church struggle it seemed to him to display a dangerous tendency to compromise with the official church authorities sponsored by National Socialism; certainly 'Faith and Order' increasingly became the domain of Bonhoeffer's enemies in Berlin, like Bishop Heckel.

There were other reasons which made him join the World Alliance and hold on to it, in spite of its theological barrenness, reasons which arose out of a reaction against the German nationalism of the early thirties which clamoured ever more loudly against pacifist-inclined organizations. Even great theologians like Hirsch and Althaus were among such nationalists. In the United States Bonhoeffer had discovered the Christian pacifism of the Sermon on the Mount, and though the Americans had not been able to teach him any theology, they certainly had taught him a commitment to the world-wide question of peace. Thus the nationalistic self-sufficiency of the 'German Christians' roused Bonhoeffer's opposition. The issue of peace in Germany became such an important matter to him that he took upon himself the difficult task of improving on the poor theology in this inter-national Alliance, and stuck to it from 1931. Thus the commitment to peace in the Alliance and the heated nationalism of the

Christian majority in Germany bound him to this issue and this organization in a positive as well as in a negative way.

Nowadays it can hardly be imagined that ecumenism at that time concerned only a minority, and that it was practically outlawed, as something to do with 'decadent internationally-minded democrats' – an effective, powerful word of insult describing the alleged enemies of national pride.

Bonhoeffer, however, did not envisage a liberal-minded internationalism. He immediately set to work, struggling to uncover the theological basis for the one universal Church in this movement too, a basis laid by the lordship of Christ. In the conference of the summer of 1932 he almost overtaxed his listeners, assuring them continually that the World Alliance was in reality different from what they believed it to be:

> The World Alliance is the alarmed and anxious Church of Christ that has pricked up its ears and, frightened by the labouring world, calls upon the Lord.[4]

Or,

> if the ecumenical movement stems from a new self-understanding of the Church of Christ, it must and will produce a theology . . . Because there is no theology of the ecumenical movement, ecumenical thought has become powerless and meaningless, especially among German youth, because of the political upsurge of nationalism.[5]

Thus Bonhoeffer established three points at issue which are still controversial today, and which coincide on the question of authenticity: the claim of the Church, the problem of passing resolutions, and the idea of a universal council determining a true confession of faith.

Firstly, ecumenism can only work and live in so far as it derives its origin from the Church of Christ and aims at being the Church. This was more than the officials of the ecumenical organizations were able to say at that time. In other words, the ecumenical movement of the World Alliance did not exist merely in order to further inter-Church and international friendships (these too, of course, were important, and Bonhoeffer was an expert at them), or only to work for peaceful and charitable issues, or just to create theological understanding through discussion and research (though Bonhoeffer was a dexterous and well-informed fighter in such matters). No, the claim and source of all organizing needed greater depth. The ecumenical movement had to understand itself as expressing a search for 'a new understanding of the nature of the Church of Christ'. The ecumenical movement is

> not an *ad hoc* organization for church action, but a definite form of the Church itself.[6]

The second line pursued by Bonhoeffer in every conference before 1933 was to fight against the tendency to pass resolutions. If the World Alliance, he asked again and again, in assuming a certain shape of the Church, expresses Christ's claim to the world,

> on what authority does the Church speak in proclaiming the claim of Christ to the world?

> How can the command be proclaimed with authority, that is, in the fullest concreteness? This is an extraordinarily difficult and important problem.[7]

If such a command cannot be given, the ecumenical Church had better be silent.

> Qualified silence might perhaps be more appropriate for the Church today than talk which is very unqualified.[8]

Here a thought reappears which we shall encounter later in the prison letters in the new formula of 'arcane discipline'. With such questions Bonhoeffer opposed, up to the end of 1932, the Anglo-Saxon readiness to pass resolutions, which seemed to him a throwing away of words in a mere general expression of opinions.

But from 1933 he all at once insisted on the ecumenical movement passing resolutions as a matter of course, for now a clear and unambiguous command had to be given in the name of Christ. It was the command concerning the problem of race, and of a false church government.

> Out of its knowledge . . . the Church must here and now be able concretely to speak the word of God, the word of power, or it will say something else, something different and human, the word of impotence. The Church must announce no eternally valid principles, but merely commandments that are valid today. For what is 'always' true is not true 'today'. To us God is 'always' God 'today'.[9]

Authority, authentic speech, cannot be enforced by anything except the command of God himself. There is no other support for it. And in the last resort, there is no other protection against the reproach of enthusiasm.

> The Church must know that and abandon all attempts to justify God's commandment. It delivers it, and that is all.[10]

Thirdly, in this struggle for an ecumenical theology determined by Christ and the Church, Bonhoeffer in 1932 used a word which at that time no Anglo-Saxon and hardly any German was prepared to accept, a word which had disappeared from Protestant terminology: 'heresy'. He must have felt even then that a situation was arising when decisions about doctrine and heresy were needed once again, because the Church had betrayed the Christ, and false Christs assumed his place. Indeed, in such a situation Bonhoeffer believed that a new epoch had begun to dawn for ecumenism.

2. ECUMENISM AND THE CONFESSING CHURCH

Two years after such reflections had been expressed by Bonhoeffer at the Youth Conference of the World Alliance, ecumenism faced a decisive hour when the World Alliance and 'Life and Work' met at Fanö in August 1934. At that time the church struggle in Germany had already experienced its first climax. Decisions were required as to whether Christians wished to belong to a Church in Germany which in full freedom acknowledged Christ as her only Lord and hence practised fellowship with all men, or else to a Church combining the Gospel of Christ with a pagan nationalistic religiosity in a new syncretism, which would also betray humanism. The Confessing Church had made her decision. Could the ecumenical movement be silent? Did it not have to take up a final position too, and thus become more than a movement?

The position was complicated and the outcome by no means a matter of course. A number of members, especially of 'Faith and Order', stated their opinion with a certain formal justification and with all the wisdom of responsible leaders of a not very powerful federal organization. They declared that internal German and internal ecclesiastical conflicts must not be tampered with from outside, and on no account prematurely; the situation was not yet clear, and was far too complicated. Inside Germany, however, the same argument was raised by the neutrally-minded and by certain church officials who were supported by the National-Socialist propaganda, which reacted violently to all outside influences.

And yet a surprising thing happened. The Fanö conference was willing to take a clear stand in favour of the Confessing Church:

> If it did not concern the ecumenical movement that a hard struggle was going on in Germany for the purity and truth of the Christian message, then no real church fellowship existed, no Christian solidarity, no mutual sharing of responsibility and suffering. The meeting at Fanö took a definite stand about the church struggle. That was a decision of tremendous importance for the whole future of the ecumenical movement.[11]

The resolution, passed under the leadership of a few men like Bishop Bell of Chichester, had been prepared with the help of Bonhoeffer. He was not in the least impressed by the reasons for opposing a so-called 'interference' as contained in the constitutions of the ecumenical associations. On the contrary, now was the time for ecumenism to represent the universal Church and stand her ground against powerful German propaganda. He looked for help from people like Bishop Ammundsen in Denmark.

It's possible that our side may be terribly cautious for fear of seeming unpatriotic . . .

In my opinion a resolution ought to be taken – no good can come of evasion . . . The only thing that can help us now is *complete truth* and *complete truthfulness*. I know that many of my German friends think otherwise. But I do beg you to consider this thought.[12]

After Fanö had spoken, Bonhoeffer considered the conference as the beginning of the 'second stage' in the history of the ecumenical movement:

The evangelical ecumenical world has never been so much in evidence on the occasion of a church dispute.[13]

Thus ecumenism had testified

first, that the struggle of the Confessing Church is bound up with the whole preaching of the Gospel, and secondly, that the struggle has been brought to a head and undergone by the Confessing Church vicariously for all Christianity, and particularly for western Christianity.[14]

This was unusual

because an understanding of ecumenical work might *a priori* have been least expected in the circles of the Confessing Church, and an interest in the theological questioning of the Confessing Church might *a priori* have been least expected in ecumenical circles.[15]

And so in this way

just as the ecumenical movement is led to a serious inward concern and crisis by the Confessing Church, so too the Confessing Church is led to a serious inward concern and crisis by the ecumenical movement,[16]

that is, the crisis of whether ecumenism was, and wanted to be, the Church, and hence whether it could make decisions which carried authority, and whether the Confessing Church could be ecumenical if she insisted on her uncompromising confession.

In an essay written after Fanö Bonhoeffer renewed his hope for an ecumenical council which, in unity and truth, and hence with a new authority, would repudiate war, racial hatred and exploitation. The official history of the ecumenical movement by Rouse and Neill has accepted Visser 't Hooft's positive judgement:

> The biennial meeting of the Council at Fanö, Denmark, during the last week of August 1934, stands out as perhaps the most critical and decisive meeting in its history. Here the Council solemnly resolved to throw its weight on the side of the Confessing Church in Germany against the so-called 'German Christians' and by implication against the Nazi regime.[17]

But Fanö did not carry the day as clearly as that, partly because the Confessing Church herself did not keep up her claim, and partly because ecumenism lost the clarity it had had at Fanö. The day came when the Confessing Church had to retreat from the field in Geneva and from the conferences preparing for the formation of the World Council of Churches, and leave it to the official church government in Germany, which still denied the right of the ecumenical movement to interfere in internal German disputes. And most of the leading men of ecumenism avoided a decision, above all a decision which would result in a rupture with the official church authorities in Berlin. But this was what Bonhoeffer demanded. He really believed that the ecumenical organizations had to risk their own existence, otherwise they would have no justification, and their proclamation would no longer be authentic.

When the organizer of 'Faith and Order' invited him to a meeting in Denmark in 1935, Bonhoeffer refused to come if the so-called Reich Church were also to be present. An exciting correspondence ensued between Bonhoeffer and the secretary of 'Faith and Order', Canon L. Hodgson. From this it became evident how the correct neutrality of most ecumenical leaders boosted the National-Socialist-supported Reich Church and eliminated the Confessing Church from the ecumenical developments by administratively throttling her.

Bonhoeffer did not give up, but in his great essay on ecumenism, which he wrote soon after this, he said that if the Confessing Church were to abandon her demand it would mean 'that the German church struggle was already decided against her, and with it the struggle for Christianity'.[18] Bonhoeffer's essay was practically ignored and was hence without effect. When in 1939 the Confessing Church, once again through Bonhoeffer, in an even more desperate plight, applied to 'Faith and Order' in London for help, the unintentional condemnation of her existence was repeated by the correct legalism of the board of directors. It was clear that Bonhoeffer had always been asking too much for their liking; or else the ecumenical organization had shirked its great hour, as Bonhoeffer himself thought.

> The question of the Confessing Church has led us beyond the necessary stage of theological discussion only.[19]

Theological discussion had become a tool used by the Reich Church to keep ecumenism busy with preliminaries in an attempt to prevent it taking the vital decision about the Church, and in this the constitution of the organization was on the Reich Church's side.

For Bonhoeffer, ecumenism was no longer merely a meeting of Christian personalities or a council of theologians. It meant for him the assembly of the Church of Christ witnessing to the Church of Christ. If anybody insisted on first defining the nature of the Church, he regarded this as a refusal to *be* the Church *now*. As early as 1934 he had written to Pastor Henroid, Secretary of the World Alliance in Geneva, with passionate conviction:

> A decision has got to be taken some time, and it's no good waiting indefinitely for a sign from heaven that will solve the difficulty without further trouble. Even the ecumenical movement has to make up its mind . . . To delay or fail to make decisions may be more sinful than to make wrong decisions out of faith and love . . . Should the ecumenical movement fail to realize this, and if there are none who are 'violent to take heaven by force', Matt. 11:12, then the ecumenical movement is no longer Church, but a useless association fit only for speechifying . . . We must shake off our fear of the Word – the cause of Christ is at stake, and are we to be found sleeping?
>
> . . . And if all the 'wise', the old and the influential are unwilling to act with us and are held back by all kinds of considerations – then it is you who must attack, you who must advance. Don't let yourself be stopped or misled; after all, if we're really honest with ourselves, we do know in this case what is right and what is wrong. Someone has got to show the way, fearlessly, and unflinchingly – why not you? For there's much more at stake than just people or administrative difficulties – Christ is looking down at us and asking whether there is anyone who still confesses him.[20]

In the end a rupture occurred between Bonhoeffer and the official committees in Geneva. A committee meeting of the Youth Commission in London in February 1937 was the last official ecumenical meeting in which Bonhoeffer took part. It ended on a wrong note.

> I realize that things cannot go on this way. It is highly unsatisfactory for you as well as for me. We must make a change for the sake of the cause. I must resign my post.[21]

Bonhoeffer's faith in ecumenism, however, did not end, it only changed. And a person now emerged in the ecumenical world who understood him and did not abandon his cause, Visser 't Hooft. But before Bonhoeffer started on a new phase of ecumenical work, he was to undergo a decisive experience. His ecumenical relations assumed a private character which later determined the public one.

3. FORSAKING ECUMENISM FOR ITS OWN SAKE

Bonhoeffer experienced an ecumenical disappointment when he tried to emigrate from Germany in 1939. For a man like Bonhoeffer the idea of emigration had, since 1933, been ever present at the back of his mind, either as a possibility or as a potential necessity. His ministry in London in 1933 had been a first attempt at escape. But he had immediately obeyed the call of the Confessing Church to run the preachers' seminary at Finkenwalde, sacrificing alluring plans to travel to India. During his time in London the fate of immigrants had been one of his main concerns. While he was recalling his experiences with so many of these people, his theological students at Finkenwalde had been rather enthusiastic in their praise of some of the courageous actions of Confessional synods, synods which had not even considered the emigrations and their causes. The Churches had been silent when Professor Siegmund-Schultze, the great man of the World Alliance, had been chased out of the country, and when Barth had had to leave the University of Bonn.

Up to 1938 Bonhoeffer had not allowed the idea of his own possible emigration to dominate his thoughts. But gradually even his own groups within the Confessing Church began to crumble away; young candidates submitted to the so-called 'Reich Church'; most ministers of the Confessing Church took the unscrupulous oath of allegiance to Hitler after his invasion of Austria; the Confessing Church allowed herself to be forced into publicly denouncing Barth after his famous letter to Hromádka in which he wrote that every Czech soldier who fought against Hitler's invasion was doing so for the cause of Christ; and the

Confessing Church was silent about the 'Crystal Night'. The Leibholz family[22] had to leave the country in a hurry because a new order about passports for Jews threatened to abolish their freedom of movement. And lastly, the time was approaching when Bonhoeffer, in the course of the rapidly increasing recruitments, would himself be conscripted.

> I am thinking of leaving Germany sometime. The main reason is the compulsory military service to which men of my age (1906) will be called up this year. It seems to me conscientiously impossible to join in a war under the present circumstances. On the other hand the Confessing Church as such has not taken any definite attitude in this respect and probably cannot take it as things are. So I should cause a tremendous damage to my brethren if I would make a stand on this point . . . *and yet there are only very few friends who would approve of my attitude.*[23]

Like everybody else, Bonhoeffer clearly foresaw that the Confessing Church would suffer Hitler's war to happen without objection and opposition, and might even participate in it.

Why should he not leave his country now, and his Church, and devote himself to his passion, theology, in a place which offered him the opportunity, namely the ecumenical movement? Had he not always struggled to be a Christian of the universal Church first and foremost? Had his priority not been: Church – Germany; and not the other way round: Germany – Church? And now he was being offered the opportunity in the United States, with no difficulties in the way, by Reinhold Niebuhr and Paul Lehmann.

So he went to the United States. But he was hardly there when he realized the truth, amidst a kind of disappointment. The old priorities did not fit any longer. A debt had accumulated for every German, which had to be paid off. And his own Church had not kept what she had received, or rather had never achieved what in her protest she had once promised: 'If necessary, to put a spoke into the wheel'. And what about the ecumenical movement? It too had not managed to achieve the universal Protestant council which was to proclaim its conflict with the state of injustice and call upon people to bear the consequences and 'protect the State from itself and preserve it as a state'.[24] Certainly, the ecumenical movement in the United States was well able to save a good friend from Germany and even grant him the unique privilege of adequate work, in preference to thousands of immigrants. But as for the Christians in Germany in their hopeless situation, for which they too bore some responsibility, they could do no more than save a few single ones like him. Bonhoeffer realized this, and the thought was unbearable.

We possess his diary from those days in the United States, and this allows us to share the struggle in his heart:

> 30th June: I cannot think it is God's will that, if war comes, I am to stay here with no special task. I must go on the earliest possible date . . .
>
> That was a great decision . . .
>
> All day long the situation in Germany and the Church has been on my mind.[25]

This passage clearly reveals the change in priorities. Ecumenism had taken second place; it would regain priority only if he shared responsibility now for Germany and her situation, and if he refused to profit from the privileges offered by ecumenism. He might, later on, become ecumenically active and effective once again. Who dares judge and condemn Bonhoeffer for joining the conspiracy against Hitler with its ambiguous consequences? Neither the Confessing Church, whose failure drove Bonhoeffer to take this step, nor the ecumenical movement can do so. Both of them disappointed Bonhoeffer and embarked him on the course of action by which he tried to change the situation in his country.

The brief and momentous attempt at emigration in 1939 had meanwhile given Bonhoeffer a fresh view of ecumenism which he had not had until then.

> Perhaps I have learnt more in this month than in the whole year nine years ago.[26]

During the short space of time he was in the United States Bonhoeffer learnt to understand parts of the Protestant Church in America afresh, namely the Free Churches, and experienced something specific of their inner life, thought and structure.

America had once been the classic country of refugees, people who had escaped a final struggle and therefore had been able to give tolerance a determining place in their own creed. Bonhoeffer now saw this more clearly and wrote a paper about it called 'Protestantism without Reformation'.[27] In this paper his ecclesiology is as Christocentric as ever. But historical conditions are seen in a more sophisticated way than before, and sociological facts are taken into account. Thus the themes of freedom and refuge are based on direct experience and assume a different form:

> To hold out to the last may be commanded, to flee may be allowed, perhaps even demanded. The Christian's flight in persecution does not of itself mean apostasy and disgrace, for God does not call everyone to martyrdom. Not fleeing but denial is sin; that is to say that there may be a situation in which flight amounts to denial, just as on the other hand flight can be an act of martyrdom . . . The Christian refugee has claimed the right to avoid the final suffering, in order to be able to serve God in peace and quietness. But at the place of refuge the continuation of the struggle is no longer justified . . . His demand for a decision for the truth against its falsification is unfulfilled and must remain so. It is finally the truth against one's own church history which is expressed in this unique relativizing of the question of truth in the thought and actions of American Christianity.[28]

In spite of his new understanding, however, Bonhoeffer remained critical of the American ideology of freedom:

> The essential freedom of the Church is not a gift from the world to the Church, but is the freedom of the Word of God itself to get a hearing . . . Where thanks for institutional freedom have to be rendered by sacrificing freedom of

preaching, the Church is in chains, even if it thinks it is free.[29]

Such questions were not raised to weaken ecumenism, but on the contrary to strengthen it:

What is God doing to us and with his Church in America, and what is he doing through it to us, and through us to it?[30]

The answer to that question required a realistic and fruitful partnership. Each Church must be able to say in what way it wants to be questioned by the others. The Churches of the Reformation in Europe, in order to be understood, wish to be questioned on the basis of their confession in relation to their break with Rome. The American denominations, which have inherited but not produced this act of schism, must be understood and questioned on the basis of the schism which is no longer to be maintained.

Thus, with new insights about his own destiny and a broadened view of ecumenism, Bonhoeffer returned to Germany, without blaming either one side or the other. When war began, he accepted the judgement of responsibility for his country, its state of affairs, and its deeds. He accepted the judgement for himself too:

Since I have been on board, the inward disharmony about the future has ceased, and I can think without any reproaches about the shortened time in America. *Losung:* 'It is good for me that I was afflicted, that I might learn thy statutes', Psalm 119:71. One of my favourite passages from my favourite psalm.[31]

There is no doubt that this decision to return, which for the time being was taken against the ecumenical movement, is the most significant reason why Bonhoeffer has become an ecumenical figure. His witness for Christ and for his community all over the world was given a new authenticity. Only when he proleptically took upon himself the guilt of his nation and confessed to it, did the freedom of the Gospel unfold again.

4. MISUSING ECUMENISM

During the war Bonhoeffer's share in the conspiracy and masquerade needed for planning the overthrow of the Nazis endangered his relationship with the ecumenical movement tremendously. Only a very small group of people saw and understood what was happening. Naturally such matters could not be dealt with, nor officially supported, by a committee. Bonhoeffer had to make his ecumenical connections look quite ambiguous and serve as a camouflage. For on the one hand he served as an agent for Hitler's war and might rightly be supposed to have betrayed the ecumenical cause. And in fact he did represent his case like that during his interrogations at Tegel prison in order to protect his friends outside:

> I made a great sacrifice . . . namely the offering of all my ecumenical connections for military use.[32]

On the other hand, Bonhoeffer could and did rely entirely on his partners like Visser 't Hooft and Bishop Bell to understand what was happening. In fact a wealth of trust proved to be there, and available for use. Visser 't Hooft and George Bell knew how to be silent when necessary, and how to trust completely. They cooperated because their partner was worthy of trust after everything that had gone on before, and because the matter at stake promised a future.

> . . . this spirit of fellowship and of Christian brotherliness will carry me through the darkest hour, and even if things go worse than we hope and expect, the light of these few days will never extinguish in my heart . . . I shall think of you on Wednesday. Please pray for us.[33]

Bonhoeffer was able to send greetings to Bell once again. It was on the last day of his life in Schönberg, on 8 April 1945. Shortly after hearing it, Bell carefully wrote down what Bonhoeffer's fellow-prisoner Captain Best told him. These may really have been Bonhoeffer's last words to ecumenism. Bell's notes tell them a little differently from the way they are usually quoted:

> Tell him [he said] that for me this is the end but also the beginning. With him I believed in the principle of our Universal Christian brotherhood which rises above all national interests, and that our victory is certain – tell him too that I have never forgotten his words at our last meeting.[34]

In a memorial service in London in July 1945 Bell bore testimony to Bonhoeffer, saying that his withdrawal from ecumenism and his sacrifice of his own reputation are in truth to be understood as genuine martyrdom:

> As one of a noble company of martyrs of differing traditions, he represents both the resistance of the believing soul, in the name of God, to the assault of evil, and also the moral and political revolt of the human conscience against injustice and cruelty. He and his fellows are indeed built upon the foundation of the Apostles and the Prophets. And it was this passion for justice that brought him, and so many others . . . into such close partnership with other resisters, who, though outside the Church, shared the same humanitarian and liberal ideals . . .
>
> For him . . . there is the resurrection from the dead; for Germany redemption and resurrection . . .; for the Church, not only in that Germany which he loved, but the Church Universal which was greater to him than nations, the hope of a new life.[35]

Thus Bonhoeffer's martyrdom has become an eminently ecumenical martyrdom and a foundation-stone for the authenticity of ecumenism. At all times such an authenticity has been the meaning of martyrdom.

FOUR

The Dilemma of Exile

I. THE CHURCH AND EXILE

The long list of eminent German exiles from all walks of life from 1933 onwards does not contain the name of one ecclesiastic. Certainly, Paul Tillich and Karl-Ludwig Schmidt belong to the ranks of the first and great refugees of the year 1933, but they undoubtedly take their place more among the persecuted university teachers than among the churchmen. It was not for the sake of their theology that they had to retreat. There was scarcely any theology in the books which Goebbels delivered up for burning in front of the universities on 10 May 1933. And professors of theology were still able to write and publish in the Third Reich for a fairly long time. It was as politically 'left-wing' professors that Tillich and Schmidt had to give up their official positions and leave Germany. It must be said of Tillich that in 1933 he neither hoped for or demanded anything from the Protestant Church for himself or his work.

With Karl Barth it was a different matter. He was waiting for a call from the Church – already at that time the Confessing Church – when in 1935 the Minister of Education expelled him from his chair at Bonn University. Barth was ready to run the risk of remaining, under commission from the Church, but the call failed to materialize. In 1935 the National Synod of the Confessing Church in Augsburg showed relief when it succeeded in keeping the uncompromising, political Barth away from the conference. On his departure, Barth wrote to his friend Hermann Albert Hesse, moderator of the Reformed Federation, that he was disturbed that the Confessing Church 'still has no heart for millions of victims of injustice. It has not yet found one word for the simplest questions of public integrity. When it does speak, it continues to talk only of its own affairs.' The German Church cannot hold up Barth as one of its great exiles – even if it wanted to. It was too relieved to be freed from identification with this Swiss theologian!

From 1937, as the noose of the 'Aryan clause' was ever more rigorously tightened, a refugee movement began which now seized men of the Church as well. A number, exceedingly small to be sure, of 'racially' trapped church officials had to go into exile and seek new avenues of employment. Among the first was Bonhoeffer's closest friend, Franz Hildebrandt (assistant pastor to Martin Niemöller in Berlin-Dahlem), who, after Niemöller's arrest, had to retreat in great haste. The German congregation in London (led by their pastor, Dr Julius Rieger) offered Hilde-brandt refuge, but as a result had to put up with censure and the erection of financial obstacles by the Church's External Affairs Office in Berlin. Among other members of this group of exiles were the Westphalian pastor and former philosophy professor Hans Ehrenberg, and the Pomeranian pastor Dr Kurt Meschke. It also included, in the course of the next year, a group of thirty-one pastors whom the Bishop of Chichester, George Bell, brought to England on his own responsibility.

Once again this was a kind of unburdening for the Church in Germany, which had done so little to make emigration possible for these exiles. Previously few had really dared to sacrifice anything for this incriminating group of their colleagues. But by this time things had changed so much that the word 'emigrant', which till then had been considered a term of abuse to nationally-minded Christians, now appeared to many to indicate an almost desirable status – of course with no real conception of what this status might mean. However, this was a later stage of development which did not bring about any far-reaching change in the general attitude to the phenomenon of exile.

During the years 1933 and 1934 men of the Church – from the ranks both of the official and of the opposing Confessing Church – did not under any circumstances want to be identified with or even seen with the taboo emigrants in Prague, Paris, or London.

When Friedrich Siegmund-Schultze, the first great ecumenist of German Protestantism, had to leave Germany in June of 1933 on Hitler's own instigation, few in the Church came to the defence of this 'internationalist and pacifist', as collaborators in the World Alliance for Promoting International Friendship through the Churches were then labelled by the newspapers. The head of the Church External Affairs Office, Bishop Theodor Heckel, reproachfully warned his German pastors abroad that their opposition to Ludwig Müller's authority in the Church aligned them without question with the 'Prague emigrants' – and for nationally-minded church people at the time this was a particularly offensive and dangerous label. But the Confessing Church also went to the greatest trouble to protect the purity of its struggle from any connection with the emigrants – and a wealth of evidence can be produced to support this fact.

Among the many factors which stood in the way of a more positive attitude toward the emigrants, the weak stance of the Church with respect to the Jewish question is of course especially important.[1] It was a stance which had its theological, political, and nationalistic reasons, and which only allowed the Church to react very slowly and late – too late!

In 1933 Bishop Marahrens had Licentiate Leo, his 'show-piece pastor' of Jewish origin, write him a testimonial, in which even this victim testified to the bishop that Jewry had been the cause of certain damage to the thoroughly Christian culture of the German people, and that the Jews 'would have to acknowledge the measures of the authorities as long as they were not servile to them in their consciences'.

In Berlin-Steglitz in September 1935 the Confessing Synod of the Old Prussian Union was unable (two weeks after the proclamation by the Nazi Party Congress of the discriminatory Nuremberg laws) to formulate any pronouncement against the degradation of a group of fellow-citizens. The activities of the organization for the aid of refugees initiated by Superintendent, later Professor, Martin Albertz in Berlin (an organization which after 1937 became known under commission from the Confessing

Church as the Grüber Office) must, when seen in context, be classified as a minimal exception to the rule. The Protestant Church, including the Councils of Brethren of the Confessing Church, could not and would not ever publicly confess this aid for exiles. And public declaration would hardly have helped the effectiveness of whatever aid was given at that time. But this is not yet the whole truth.

Even in the Churches of the neighbouring countries, understanding and help for the exiles remained more limited than is commonly accepted. The names of the exceptions acquired a disproportionately widespread good repute, at the time gratefully passed on in whispers by those concerned. Today they are loudly acclaimed by those who collect 'plus points' for the Church, and yet they were scarcely noticed by the majority of the emigrants. Certainly, what they achieved did not decisively change the reputation of the Churches.

That is not just my observation. The biography of Bishop George Bell, in its deeply moving chapters about his fight for the refugees, contains an account of the failure at that time. In 1937 Bell noted:

> It is humiliating, but it is true . . . the Christian Churches in England and elsewhere have made the minutest response. There have been individual Christians who have been generous. But the Churches as a whole are silent, and, it seems, unconcerned.

In 1938 he wrote:

> It is almost as hard to understand the seeming apathy with which the fate of the Jews and the non-Aryan Christians is being regarded by the people of the British Empire . . . These non-Aryans can no longer be called 'refugees' for they have as yet no countries of refuge.[2]

In 1939 Bell finally admitted that the Churches had done more than they had previously; but by now the refugee problem had taken on such huge dimensions that voluntary groups were totally unable to cope with it. Having taken his seat in the House of

Lords in 1938, Bell declared that if decisive steps were not taken by the Government, and the problem was allowed to fester, then 'it will poison our whole civilization'.

In fact the problem did poison our civilization – by which Bell meant 'the Christian West' – and the consequences have not yet been overcome. At this point, one might ask, does forgetting bring about a real healing of the wound or only self-deception? In spite of Grüber and Bell, the Church and those in exile had little to do with each other. Great Christians play no part in exilic literature, and great exiles had little to write about Churches and Christians. And what are the Churches writing about exile today?

In its quest for an authentic Christianity and a suitable form for the Church, has 'modern' German theology really rediscovered and presented the idea of pilgrimage in the wilderness and in exile as the 'classical' form of biblical existence for the children of God?

An examination of the most recent Protestant encyclopedia reveals suspicious deficiencies in this regard. An inspection of key words such as 'emigration', 'banishment', 'deportation', 'exile', 'refugees' and 'expulsion' suggests a negative answer to the question we are asking. For example, in the *Evangelische Kirchenlexikon* the article on 'Exile' describes the Babylonian captivity of Israel six centuries before Christ. 'Emigration' deals with refugees from Eastern Europe after 1945. 'Refugees' tells about the history of the Huguenots, and about 'displaced persons' in post-war Europe. 'Expulsion' also refers to 'displaced persons', and there is no section on 'Banishment'. Even the articles on 'Anti-Semitism' and 'Jewry', though accurate, do not deal with exile in the way we mean it. The position presented in *Religion in Geschichte und Gegenwart* is not very different. Here 'emigration' is dealt with in terms of political economy; 'refugees' refers to migrant workers and displaced persons. What seems most surprising is that the *Evangelische Staatslexikon*, which appeared more recently, makes no mention of the problem of exile during the Third Reich under any of its pertinent headings. It refers to 'alien rights' in a strictly legal manner; it deals with ecumenical church refugee aid only after 1948; and in a lengthy article on the 'Right to a Homeland', it recalls in one very general sentence that: 'The criminal violations committed by the Third Reich with regard to deportations and mass expulsions are on a par with the counterblows aroused by them.' But the real problem of the 'exile' and 'refugee' hardly appears. There is no description of the post-1933 state of political-religious and racist persecution which had exile as its aim, and which struck at democrats, communists, scholars, artists, Jews and Christians alike.

In the meantime the Churches in Germany have vigorously taken up the cause of 'displaced persons', but without coming to grips with the problem of 'exile'. Chancellor Konrad Adenauer was successful in labelling his political opponent Willie Brandt as an 'exile' in a way that was disparaging. At celebrations of the political resistance, official speakers emphasize more strongly their distance from everything which inevitably led into the area of the acknowledged 'treason', and conveniently forget that the conspirators against the Third Reich had to look for and cultivate connections with foreign exile groups. And this kind of thinking has affected the Churches, thus prompting the question which we have already asked, and must ask again: Has it not once again been demonstrated in the history of the Church that it is more committed to 'settledness' than it is to showing any solidarity with the uprooted wanderer?

Baalim, the gods of nature and homeland, were always more tempting than Jahweh, the impoverished God of the desert and the exile. Similarly, the diaspora existence of the early Christian congregations soon gave way to their establishment as recognized protectors and preservers of morality in the static established society. This fact is reflected in our church language through the use of the Greek word '*parochia*'. 'Parochial' or 'parish' are words which today express the very opposite of that which their biblical origin conveyed. Abraham, the typically biblical exile, was the '*paroikos*' (Septuagint), that is, the stranger. His obedience in faith consisted in his becoming '*paroikos*', an exile.

In early Christendom the concepts '*ekklesia*' and '*paroikia*' were interchangeable and described the alien quality of Christianity. The Letter to the Hebrews in particular uses the image of the movable and temporary tent when it speaks about the Christian community, and it refers to Jesus and his own as 'outside the city gate'. But then the word '*ekklesia*' slowly became a designation for the Church as a whole, and the word '*paroikia*' became the title for the individual congregation. From '*paroikia*' came the idea of a parish, an established residential area. Instead of the idea of 'strangers and pilgrims on earth', the emphasis began to be placed on settled lives of tranquillity and quietness. Eventually, the established parish became the support of civic order, it was used to justify various nationalisms, and even became a component in the theological rationalization for the 'right to a homeland'. And suddenly, in Germany in the 1930s, the parish's missionary responsibility to the settled congregation, and its concern for and ministry to exiles became mutually exclusive. It was argued with persuasion that the Church should concentrate on its ministry to the mass of society to which it had ready access, on a ministry for which it had political support, and not jeopardize this missionary opportunity by taking a stand on behalf of people who were in danger of becoming exiles.

The issue becomes clearer when we compare the way in which the Church in Germany responded to the problem of 'displaced persons'. The Church performed, and is still performing, tremendous and perceptive relief work for displaced persons in Europe and elsewhere. But exile and displacement are not the same thing. True exiles would not want to be confused with displaced persons, and the latter would not want to be mentioned in the same breath with exiles! A comparison of the two types makes the difference between them more evident:

(i) Exile belongs among the causes of the Second World War, displacement among its results.

(ii) Exile implies being excommunicated from the hitherto existing historical unit of people and language. Displacement implies being dislodged from the hitherto existing residential, geographical unit, but it does not entail ex-communication from the historical unit of people and language.

(iii) The exile is tied by his native language to his mortal enemy and separated by it from his new friends. But native language separates the displaced person from his enemies and joins him to his friends.

(iv) The exile is a living reproach to his native country – better to overlook and conceal him. The displaced person is a living reproach to the outside world – he is to be exhibited and spoken of as loudly as possible. The position of the exile creates or demands self-examination, self-analysis, self-knowledge; that of the displaced persons encourages self-pity.

Under the spotlight of the problem of exile, the dilemma of the Church with regard to its self-understanding is uncovered or confirmed.

2. BONHOEFFER – EXILE

What was Dietrich Bonhoeffer's attitude to exile, to refugees, to the possibility of his own emigration, and to co-operation with the exiles?

At the beginning of the Third Reich, three factors made Bonhoeffer immediately more critical of 'Blood and Earth' theories and practices than many of his colleagues in the university faculty and in the Church. Firstly, for his age and considering the conditions of the time, he had a remarkable number of foreign experiences and ecumenical encounters behind him. They immediately caused him to react most sensitively against the rising provincialism of Church and State. Three times he tried to visit India and experience life there, with a desire stretching beyond normal curiosity. He saw such a visit as providing an opportunity to move beyond the bounds of his European, Western Christen-

dom. Secondly, his intense friendship with Franz Hildebrandt
(the theologian of half-Jewish origin) and the fate threatening his
brother-in-law Gerhard Leibholz allowed him to see immediately
the consequences for the State and the Church, which the men of
the Church, thoroughly pleased with the anti-Bolshevism of the
Third Reich, would not take seriously. And finally, his theological thinking in the two years preceding 1933 had already
begun to incorporate the exilic element in Christian faith, the
alienation of discipleship. He began, therefore, not with Paul's
Letter to the Romans, as Protestant renewals usually do, but
rather with the Sermon on the Mount, which negates any fixation
with a homeland.

Thus Bonhoeffer did things at the onset of the Third Reich
period which did not bring him any popularity. At the beginning
of 1933 the Nazi Government was seeking every German who
'in any way possesses connections abroad [so that] he can use
these in an enlightening fashion to spread the truth about the
Jewish plot of atrocity in letters, telegrams and telephone con-
versations'. On 30 March, therefore, highly placed men of the
Church wrote to all countries. For example, the President of the
German Church Federation, Hermann Kapler, wrote to Bell,
Germanos, Cadman and Henriod. Otto Dibelius and the Methodist Bishop John L. Nuelson spoke over short-wave radio to
America, asking that steps be taken to stop the agitation against
the peaceful new order of Germany. Bonhoeffer, on the other
hand, committed what was an offence, even in those days,
against Hitler's 'Treachery Law' of 21 March and gave his friend
from the United States, Paul L. Lehmann (who was visiting him
in Berlin at that time), authentic descriptions of Berlin pro-
cedures against political leftists and Jews. He was to take these
with him for the head rabbi of New York, Rabbi Wise. In the
days of the first non-Aryan law 'for the restitution of the civil
service' he wrote a discourse for Rabbi Wise on the attitude of
the Church to the Jewish question. For here, he believed, 'the
most intelligent people have totally lost their heads and their
Bibles'. It was a remarkable document. What he wanted to say

polemically he wrapped in a series of conservative sentences on the problem of State and Church – sentences of a confessed Lutheran who separated the two kingdoms far from each other.

During the period when I was giving a series of lectures on Bonhoeffer at the Chicago Theological Seminary in 1966, a professor of the University of Chicago who was a refugee from Germany quoted sentences like these in his sociology seminar, without naming the author:

> Without doubt, the Church of the Reformation has no right to address the State directly in its specifically political actions. ... Without doubt the Jewish question is one of the historical problems which our State must deal with, and without doubt the State is justified in adopting new methods here.[3]

He then asked his seminar, 'Who do you think wrote that? – none other than your beloved hero, Dietrich Bonhoeffer.' This refugee was not wrong of course. Here was a German Lutheran still preaching in a constant theological frontal position against what was for him, Bonhoeffer, simply a liberal-humanitarian environment.

At that time this kind of theological position was nothing out of the ordinary in the German Church. What did attract attention, however, was what Bonhoeffer said at the same time: (a) that the Church had to oppose the State prophetically, in that the solution of the Jewish question no longer lay within the limits of legitimate state action; (b) that the Church was duty-bound to the victims of state action, without discrimination between Christian and non-Christian; and (c) that the Church should not only care for the victims of the inexorable wheel of state machinery but should throw a wrench into the spokes of that wheel. Even if it was wrapped in a 'neat Lutheran package', this attitude generated horror in the circle of Berlin theologians to whom it was presented in April 1933. According to reports, Leonhard Fendt, the great Berlin preacher and professor of practical theology, left the circle.

Bonhoeffer's initial position placed him in a difficult dilemma.

His personal vitality, the sense of public social responsibility which he had inherited, combined with his successful start in an academic career, made it impossible for him simply to submerge silently. If there was no prospect of his still belonging to that society in which he lived, then he had to find a suitable form of exile. Although the term 'inner exile' does not completely cover the phenomenon, it would still be fairly accurate to apply it to Bonhoeffer's passage into the Church, where he looked for a kind of legitimate exile. Yet each time his exile took shape, his restless wandering would begin anew.

His stay in his first position, in a Berlin parish, was short; his stay in his second, in a foreign congregation, was a little longer. While he was disappointed over the reaction of the universities to Hitler in the spring of 1933, he still put faith in the Protestant Church, and in that turbulent summer of 1933 he expected certain appropriate actions from it. He was hoping that the pastors would give up their jobs. Together with Franz Hildebrandt, he suggested the medieval weapon of the interdict, that is, a refusal to perform official state functions like weddings and funerals, in order to make Christian people conscious of the fact that the State was pulling a fast one on the Church. This worked later in Norway in 1940–1. With Hermann Sasse he formulated a declaration that the 'German Christians' should challenge the theologians of the 'Blood and Earth' faction. When the Aryan clause was introduced into church legislation, he pleaded that the time had come for a mass exodus from this Church. But in these concerns he was virtually alone, and so in the autumn of 1933 he was glad that he could turn his back on this Church. Nevertheless he was still a little uncertain as to whether he had really always been right, since he was opposed to the great majority of his friends.

He then withdrew into a kind of quiet exile – into the pastorate of two small German parishes in London. But he completely deceived himself as to the peacefulness of his withdrawal. The more the ecumenical movement in London needed him as an interpreter, the deeper he became entangled in the struggles flaring up at home. But these struggles were now the struggles of an awakened opposition whose appearance surprised even Bonhoeffer, and which slowly organized itself into the Confessing Church.

In London he encountered the misery of exile for the first time in a direct form. 'Besides my parish work . . . I have an endless number of visitors, mostly Jews, who know me from somewhere or other and always want something.' Among such visitors there were even former cabinet ministers like the Conservative, Gottfried W. Treviranus. In the summer of 1934 Bonhoeffer called on Reinhold Niebuhr in America for help.

> To be sure, a committee was formed here recently, especially for academics, but its resources are as good as nothing. Here in London, my mind is particularly burdened by a man, twenty-three years old, former leader of the Republican Student Federation, and a lawyer. He is in real distress and I can place him nowhere. The other is the author Arnim T. Wegner – Tillich will know him I am sure. He is very left-wing, has had terrible times in a concentration camp and is totally worn out. He has been unable to find anything here and is despairing as a result. Forgive me for troubling you with these things, but this is only a tiny sample of what we see here almost daily. It reaches the point where one finally simply stands there and can no longer help. My congregations support me in the work with great understanding. This is an important assistance.[4]

When in 1935 the incorporation of the Saar approached and Bonhoeffer reckoned with a new wave of refugees, he organized a reception service in his parishes and was the force behind a memorandum on the impossible stance of England, who solemnly emphasized her tradition of being a refuge but withheld every kind of working position from the refugee. He asked Bishop Bell for help and intervention, but he had negligible success.

Similar experiences made Bonhoeffer more keenly aware of how substantially the Confessing Church as well was only concerned with her own affairs. He later judged Confessing synods by this criterion, and astounded his students when repeatedly he would not share their enthusiasm for this or that courageous synod.

In 1934 the church opposition, which in the meantime had been strengthened, demanded a new decision from Bonhoeffer – to return home:

> I am bothered about deciding where to go, either back to Germany in order to lead a preachers' seminary, or to stay here in London, or to go to India . . .
>
> And at long last a stop must be put to that reliance on would-be theological grounds concerning the actions of the State – it is in fact due simply to fear. 'Open thy mouth for the dumb' – who in the Church today acknowledges that this is the very last of the demands the Bible makes on us in these times?[5]

In 1935 at Finkenwalde a new form of his inner exile within the Church began. Though withdrawn from immediate involvement in the church struggle, the seminary was highly controversial; a centre for pastoral training which was strongly theologically orientated and which stressed daily worship, but at the same time a centre constantly attacking any compromising and self-protective steps on the part of its own Church.

It was there, too, that after 1936 Bonhoeffer took in pastors who, because of their Jewish origins or kinship, had been defeated and driven from their parishes. Where possible, he helped them on the road to foreign exile. It is possible that common sense already occasionally pointed to his own exile – as he remembered how the situation of his twin-sister and her husband had deteriorated after the passing of the Nuremberg laws. Yet any serious consideration of foreign exile still did not enter his mind in 1936-7. The controversial inner emigration within the Church still seemed to make his own integrity possible, indeed, integrity seemed to demand the inner emigration absolutely.

Something changed, however, in the dramatic year of 1938. Almost all of the Confessing pastors in office took a far too

extensive and unconditional oath to Hitler, an oath demanded
by the official church leadership, and one which had been declared
heretical by the Confessing Church. Bonhoeffer travelled among
church circles trying to prevent the pastors from taking the oath,
but without much success. Even the most loyal men of the
Councils of Brethren emphatically dissociated themselves from
Karl Barth's letter to Josef L. Hromádka, which encouraged
the Czechoslovaks to resist Hitler's annexation, and the bishops
would have nothing to do with the publication by the Councils
of Brethren of a prayer liturgy which contained prayers for the
withholding of divine judgement in the form of war during the
Czech crisis. (The *Schwarzes Korps* termed this 'treasonable
action in clerical garb'.) When the synagogues burned on the
'Crystal Night', the Confessing Church remained silent.

The ranks of Bonhoeffer's candidates crumbled. First hopes as
early as 1938 for a *coup* against Hitler, in which Bonhoeffer's
brother-in-law would have been decisively involved, were not
fulfilled. A Jewish pass regulation late in the summer of 1938 now
made the hurried emigration of his sister's family very necessary.
Bonhoeffer's own conscription into the army drew considerably
closer, and the *Bruderräte* were reluctant to take on, in addition to
the problems posed by Hromádka and the prayer liturgy, the case
of open, and at the time singular, conscientious objection to war
which the name Bonhoeffer implied. By doing so they would
forfeit the last remnant of dependability in the eyes of the
nation.

Thus thoughts of leaving Germany, which up to now had been
vague, became serious. Why should he not live out his calling,
namely 'doing theology', writing ethics, where freedom and
opportunity were offered to him by the ecumenical movement
of Western countries? Who would prevent him from seeking
self-fulfilment where he was wanted instead of staying where
people found his frightening appeals and actions uncomfortable?
The necessary invitation came in time, before a border crossing
might have become impossible for Bonhoeffer.

Doors opened for his exile in New York. The occupational

difficulties facing so many other refugees did not exist for him. And it was precisely this which contributed to giving his exile a completely different form:

> There are many other refugee pastors. I must not block the chances for them by accepting this job in the States.[6]

At this point we have a better insight than usual into Bonhoeffer's most momentous decision, because here he kept a diary for several weeks. Feelings of sheer homesickness and the pain of now having to be a German combine in these entries with a prayerful struggle for a right decision for which he could feel responsible.

> I cannot stay abroad alone. That's quite clear now. My [life] here is still at home over there.

> That short prayer in which we were remembering the brethren in Germany nearly overwhelmed me.[7]

At this moment the ecumenical refuge would have been quite a privileged place for Bonhoeffer, compared with the majority of exiles: a place in which privileged Christians would have offered a few other privileged ones an 'inter-family' shelter and the best possibilities to develop. Bonhoeffer shied away from this. But his experience of the ecumenical world was still broadened. Certainly there was noteworthy help and understanding of all kinds in the ecumenical movement, but in Bonhoeffer's view its organizations had simply failed on the great universal issues, whatever the reasons might be. On the question of the German church conflict, and likewise of exile, no one had dared to do anything decisive. Thus Bonhoeffer's emigration from German society, first into the Church, then into the ecumenical movement, had ended in monumental disappointment.

Amidst the hesitation, resistance and even excuses which his intellect, education, theological background and own physical well-being had lent weight to, the day finally came when Bonhoeffer could only remain himself by working with the ambiguous political conspiracy. Did this mean a genuine home-coming? Or was this the most extreme form of exile?

There is no doubt that the decision made in New York on 20 June 1939 ultimately changed Bonhoeffer's life down to its inmost ties. It led, for example, to his forsaking the cause of Christian pacifism. For Bonhoeffer to have pursued this further (as Hermann Stöhr did in Stettin by finally giving his life) would have meant endangering the operations of his brothers and sisters within the actively organized conspiracy. As a matter of principle, conscientious objection would have represented a somewhat private act, a kind of egocentric flight from increased responsibility and guilt. Such a stand might have appeared noteworthy, but Bonhoeffer regarded it as an act of irrelevant self-fulfilment.

The original protest character of Finkenwalde and *The Cost of Discipleship* had been forfeited, and simply to follow their concepts further became an even more abstract and personal matter. What was remarkable was the reversal which had taken place. The Church, once enthusiastically rediscovered, now only lived on sterile conceptions of survival and respectability. His brothers and sisters and friends of the family, at one time criticized as humanistic liberals, now turned to doing the necessary deeds of the Christian. One day Bonhoeffer was to think through this confusing situation theologically and also give it expression in the now famous letters from Tegel prison, *Resistance and Submission*.[8] The formula which appeared there – 'a non-religious interpretation of the Gospel in a world come of age' – also meant a theological verbalization of that return from the United States, with its inevitable consequences. No longer a return to Finkenwalde, but rather to his conspiring family and to their ethical and political payment for Germany's guilt.

The New York decision was also a homecoming, a homecoming to that self-identity which is achieved by passing through many mutations. Bonhoeffer could not stand aside and enjoy the privileges of his theological and pastoral career, whether in narrower church work or in the openness of the ecumenical movement, while brothers, in-laws and sisters risked their existence in desperate underground action.

Nevertheless it was quite a new form of 'exile'. The Lutheran teachings under the influence of which he had grown up had never yet explored the field of such actions nor worked out rules to cover it. The protection of a reliable theory, the security of church authority, had to be abandoned. Here the degrading word 'conspiracy' did not appear. But now all at once, a double life and shadowiness were supposed to be moral. Were people not failing in their duty on all sides?

By accepting the logic of conspiracy, Bonhoeffer had to allow the resistance to use him as a man of the Church, not perhaps for church or ecumenical purposes, but rather as someone who could, with the trust which he possessed in Allied countries, re-establish contacts which the resistance so desperately needed. On the other hand, he could not expect the planners to treat him as an exception, and so, like them, he had to deceive and lie. And he understood that. He did his part in spinning the web of masquerade, together with those who, without clerical privileges, kept trying to do what was necessary under ever more difficult conditions.

We have been silent witnesses of evil deeds; we have been drenched by many storms; we have learnt the arts of equivocation and pretence; experience has made us suspicious of others and kept us from being truthful and open; intolerable conflicts have worn us down and even made us cynical. Are we still of any use?[9]

Thus Bonhoeffer spoke at the time about the 'fruitful, if for now very humiliating, solution' for these times. The 'humiliating' and 'fruitful' solution? To this belonged a flight into the exile of complete incognito; up to today there has been no complete success in uncovering it.

3. BLESSINGS OF EXILE?

The dilemma 'to go or to stay' is as old as the Bible. Since biblical times it has found its solution, almost every time it presented itself, in the pain of going. Its dark, evil side has to be described, lamented and accused, as it was by the prophets, those Camuses of the Old Testament; as it was from the Cross, whose elevation in the New Testament still has not been able to eradicate fully its contingent injustice and indictment.

To speak too quickly here of God's plan – that there must always be those who force the departure of the exile and those who are forced to depart – is an inhuman and evil sort of piety. Only when a man has spared himself no questioning beforehand, only when God has sincerely been accused of this impenetrable riddle – as he is in many of the Psalms – only then perhaps can one speak of another side of the matter, of a going of necessity, of a blessed alienation.

Alienation is connected in the Bible with the concept of 'being called'. God calls to exile and to new shores. Then the 'chosen one' finds his identity and his purpose when he recognizes the call to the strange land and follows it. At first the called one scarcely knows how he will continue to live, but then he learns that he gave up his home so that he could house within himself greater and completely new and different things.

In exile in England, Bonhoeffer's niece Marianne Leibholz wrote a poem entitled 'Exile':

> And as he stood, a shaken hunted creature,
> Chased from the homeland that he loved so much,
> The sky that spread its vastness over him
> Told him there are no boundaries.
>
> Place after place he learnt to leave behind him,
> And learns in time what loneliness can mean,
> Senses the transience that shines through all,
> Pays heed and is most ready for farewells.

He gathers strength. To him no land is foreign;
His fatherland is all the sky defines.
No more, as formerly, will he come home.
He feels it thankfully. His heart is light.

The price of exile is high. The new status cannot be taken for granted for it entails going through suffering. From Switzerland, while on one of his trips for the conspiracy, Bonhoeffer wrote to his niece in England on the occasion of her confirmation: 'There are so many experiences and disappointments which drive sensitive people into the paths of nihilism and resignation. For this reason it is good to learn early that suffering and God are not contradictory, but rather form a necessary unit. For me the idea that God himself suffers has always been by far the most convincing piece of Christian teaching.'

Drawing on psychology, we can learn to express the concept of 'being called' differently: namely, as a means of establishing our true identity. One who has to leave the shelter of home reacts with the elementary fear that his identity is threatened. Exile is the most extreme threat to that identity, which nature, history and language in a specific place and context have formed. Identity is in danger of falling to pieces. It is not only seemingly threatened in exile; it can no longer remain what it was. Rather, it is only regained through painful mutation, in a complete identification with the new, which only then changes from a chaotic to an enriching force. In the fearful steps of a new identification, the gaining of a richer identity only proceeds from the loss of identity in exile. Identity destroys itself by denying its own history and is regained in accepting it.

When Bonhoeffer accepted the new identification assigned to him in 1939 in America, his return to his homeland, by which of course he wanted to be sheltered, became something more than just a return to the old identity. Now he 'accommodated' it with the new dimension of his guilt and a changed future. His previous identity grew up out of menacing alienation into a new identity. In fact he himself only now became what he had described Christ as, in a new title of majesty – a man capable 'of being there for others'.

After the war Thomas Mann, writing of the relationship between exile and life in the homeland, spoke of a 'chasm, which yawns between our experiences and those of the people left behind in Germany . . . Any understanding traversing this chasm is completely impossible.' And in 1948, referring to those who had stayed in Germany and worked against the regime, Alfred Polgar still believed that 'no name from the German intelligentsia appears among their names'. Today one is urged to see in these utterances perhaps more of a judgement about the harshness of exile than about the German resistance. Today there are members and heirs of the exile who see in the slowly unfolding incognito of Bonhoeffer's last 'inner exile' a piece of Germany which gives them cause to think again.

FIVE

Christian Political Involvement

A few years ago the Confessing Church was blamed for having exhibited a puristic timidity or fear in the face of liberal politics, and therefore for not having acted politically in a humane way.

Along with theological liberalism, the theme of humaneness was confessed away out of the Church. Along with theological liberalism, however, any relation to society in ecclesiastical theologizing was also conjured away . . .[1]

Bonhoeffer and Barth shared in this theological purism. But Barth has clearly described the other side of Bonhoeffer; he was impressed by:

Bonhoeffer's 'way from the Christian faith to political action' . . . Exactly that, however, was also my concern after my farewell to theological liberalism. It took for me the form of 'religious socialism' in its specifically Swiss appearance . . . When I began working on my *Epistle to the Romans* . . . and after I went to Germany in 1921, this concern moved out of the centre somewhat. My German hearers and readers knew me better for the attempt of mine, which was more central to my thought, to give a new interpretation of the Reformation and to make it an actuality than for that other concern. Germany, burdened with the problem of her Lutheran tradition, was very much in need of a 'refresher course' in just the outlook which I presupposed without so many words and emphasized merely in passing, namely ethics, brotherliness, a servant Church, discipleship, socialism, movements for peace – and throughout all these in politics. Obviously, Bonhoeffer sensed this void and the need to fill it with increasing urgency right from the start and gave expression to it on a very broad front. This overdue completion, for which he stood up so strongly, was and is (one hopes decisively) to a great extent the secret of the impression which he has justifiably made and is still making, especially since he became a martyr precisely for this cause.[2]

We remember Bonhoeffer's enquiry, put to Barth even before 1933, about the concrete authoritative saying and doing of the Commandment. We remember the overtones in the essay on the Jews of April 1933, the pressing for resolutions at ecumenical conferences. We remember his attempts to see Gandhi and study his passive resistance. As early as 1934 he wrote from London to his friend Erwin Sutz in Zürich, saying that the

> theologically argued reserve over against the State's actions must be broken – it is only fear, anyway. 'Open your mouth for the dumb' (Proverbs 31:8). Who in the Church still knows that this is the demand put to us by the Bible in such times? And then the question of military service, war, etc. etc. . . . I cannot understand how a man can remain in Hitler's entourage unless he is either a Nathan or else an accomplice in the guilt of the 30th of June [the Röhm blood-purge] . . . and also of the next war.[3]

The next war was drawing near, and neither had the Confessing Church opened her mouth, nor had the ecumenical movement brought about the council so ardently wished for in 1933. Instead, the monstrous war was now let loose in the name of all Germans, and the Church remained silent.

In his *Ethics*, in 1940, Bonhoeffer formulated a confession of guilt on behalf of the Church. From this we see how poignantly Bonhoeffer felt the Church's involvement in the guilt of the nation – five years before the Protestant Church in Germany actually confessed her guilt, after Germany's defeat. And even then she did so in somewhat poetical terms:

> We accuse ourselves of not having confessed more cour-

ageously, lived more loyally, believed more cheerfully, and loved more passionately.

After everything that had happened, this Stuttgart formula was short and lacking in concreteness. Bonhoeffer, however, after Hitler's greatest victory, the one over France, when it was dangerous to put anything of that kind on paper, wrote the following confession:

I am guilty of hypocrisy and untruthfulness in the face of force. I have been lacking in compassion and I have denied the poorest of my brethren.

. . . she [the Church] has often denied to the outcast and to the despised the compassion which she owes them. She was silent when she should have cried out because the blood of the innocent was crying aloud to heaven . . .

She has stood by while violence and wrong were being committed under cover of this name [Christ] . . .

She has incurred the guilt . . . of the exploitation of labour even beyond the working weekday . . .

The Church confesses that she has witnessed the lawless application of brutal force, the physical and spiritual suffering of countless innocent people, oppression, hatred and murder, and that she has not raised her voice on behalf of the victims and has not found ways to hasten to their aid. She is guilty of the deaths of the weakest and most defenceless brothers of Jesus Christ . . .

She has witnessed in silence the . . . corruption of the strong.

The Church confesses herself guilty towards the countless victims of calumny, denunciation and defamation.

. . . she has rendered herself guilty of the decline in responsible action, in bravery in the defence of a cause, and in willingness to suffer for what is known to be right.[4]

At that very time Bonhoeffer leapt from purely ecclesiastical resistance into the political conspiracy. The confession of guilt just quoted, and this leap, indicate the real crisis of the church struggle, which has not been mastered by us to this day: the crisis of the relationship between the openly proclaimed word and its authenticity, between the confession and political action in the name of humaneness, between the opposition of the Confessing Church and political opposition. This leap was not taken quickly or suddenly. The fact that Bonhoeffer thought in terms of the Lutheran concept of the ministry made such a step difficult. It was a hesitant and prolonged process which developed in three accelerating stages.

I. INFORMATION

From early 1938 members of the conspiracy worked feverishly at forming political groups capable of toppling Hitler. But the first period for Bonhoeffer was one of gathering information. It comprised the years 1938 and 1939, that is, the time before Bonhoeffer attempted to evade his difficulties by going to the United States. During this period he did not change his professional work. He continued to teach candidates of the Confessing Church. He wanted to remain a minister and study theology, and hardly thought of changing his sphere of life and work, indeed he even worried about military service. And yet the fact that he was an accessory to the plans for an overthrow of Hitler changed his life more than he admitted to himself. That he gained access to information about the conspiracy was due to his close friendship with his brother-in-law Hans von Dohnanyi, who was employed in the Ministry of Justice as a supreme-court judge.

Helmut Traub, a pupil of Karl Barth, tells us how in 1938 a circle of like-minded theologians met with Bonhoeffer in Stettin to discuss Romans 13. Traub was eager to see Bonhoeffer whom he had heard about as a radical member of the Confessing Church. This circle discussed passionately the possibilities of political opposition, and Traub tells us how disappointed he was about Bonhoeffer's silence. Afterwards, Bonhoeffer took him aside:

He assured me emphatically that he had understood me perfectly. 'But then you must be quite logical, quite different, you must go ahead in quite a different way.'[5]

'I at once realized', Traub says, 'that what I had taken for "hesitation" belonged to an entirely different category.' This incident reveals that, through being an accessory to underground political activities, Bonhoeffer was no longer able to remain in the non-committal area of harmless theoretical discussion about politics. He was deeply aware of what he might have to face, so he was silent. He knew what was really being talked about, and what the cost might be. Perhaps, too, he suspected that steps of the kind the resistance envisaged were not to be justified as a programme prepared in advance.

Bonhoeffer's political involvement acquired a new facet with the sudden emigration of his twin-sister's family, and with the threat to himself of impending conscription. His knowledge of plans for a political upheaval assumed an even more existential nature; it became a vital hope influencing his thought and action ever more strongly.

To be informed of a conspiracy was dangerous in the Third Reich. For Freisler's People's Court it later meant the death sentence. The natural curiosity of people about what was happening behind the scenes in the Third Reich had long since changed into a reluctance to know. It was better not to know too much, as any knowledge exposed one to danger. Bonhoeffer, however, never gave way to that fear. On the contrary, he took considerable pains to have access to the most exclusive and reliable information. He did not want to be deprived of what was a necessary component of his responsibility for the present time and the future. Nor did he want Hitler's sudden actions to take him by surprise. Within the sphere of his own responsibility he wished to remain as sovereign as possible, and not become a victim of something unforeseen.

The result was necessarily a kind of separation from former friends if they could not, and did not, share this level of information. Thus subjects and partners of discussions changed, and connections were formed with people whom, on theological grounds, he might once have rejected. With that, the interest in purely theoretical theological disputes waned. The priorities changed, imperceptibly at first; then they made him escape to the United States; and finally, after that attempt at flight, they were consciously rearranged.

2. READINESS

In his second period Bonhoeffer was ready to act. This was during 1939 and 1940. Externally, his style of life had still not changed completely. On the contrary, after his return from America, he devoted himself for another six months to his work with theological candidates, in spite of the war, just as if nothing had happened. There were a few months too of pastoral visiting on behalf of the Confessing Church, but Bonhoeffer's heart was no longer in the internal ecclesiastical struggle, he just did what he could for his Confessing Church. Nor was he interested any longer in assisting ecumenical travellers in their peace-making endeavours when they appeared in Germany and Berlin like the Norwegian Lutheran Bishop Berggrav who travelled backwards and forwards between Germany, Great Britain and Norway. Bonhoeffer did not even meet him in Berlin. For him there was only one course of action left. For Berggrav, and probably for Bishop Bell in England, too, the priority was: first peace, that is, prevent the great war, and then see what can be done about Hitler. For Bonhoeffer and his friends the priorities were reversed: everything must be done to eliminate Hitler first, and after that to negotiate peace. To bring this about he was prepared to help wherever he could. As a consequence, in this period of readiness, his attitudes changed.

After his return from the United States Bonhoeffer no longer propagated a practical pacifism or adopted a conscientious objection to military service as far as he personally was concerned. Before his voyage to America he had told Bell he wished to disappear from Germany because of the call-up. He had said he could not damage his weakened and defeated Confessing Church by another disastrous case, the case of Bonhoeffer the conscientious objector, burdening her with something of which she did not approve. After his return this problem had as it were vanished, it was redundant. To play the conscientious objector and the pacifist now would have meant to expose the efforts of his friends and relatives in the conspiracy to a premature discovery. When, in 1940, Hermann Stöhr of Stettin, a man whom he knew, was martyred in the name of Christ for objecting to military service, Bonhoeffer realized that he too had moved in the same direction, and so he dropped the matter. It may have appeared to him under the existing circumstances as an admirable private action, but one which entailed a refusal to share, in the name of Christ, what others in Germany had to take upon themselves. He may have realized that it was no longer a matter of keeping one's reputation clean as a Christian, a pastor and an individual, but of sacrificing everything, even one's reputation as a Christian. This reputation had disappeared long ago anyway, in the silence about the Aryan laws, the blood-purge of 30 June 1934, the 'Crystal Night' and the war. Could a person like Bonhoeffer really enjoy a privileged position, even as a martyr for pacifism, and remain aloof when his friends, his brothers and his sisters risked their lives in political action?

His attitude about saying 'Yes' or 'No' in public also changed. In earlier times he had looked for people who, in their Christian and ecclesiastical life, or in their secular and professional sphere, summoned up the courage to say 'No', thus publicly risking dismissal from their posts. Now it was of the utmost importance to put influential people at the controls if possible. Formerly, for instance, it had been a question of character whether one gave the Hitler salute, or refused to do so. Now that kind of thing became a mere bagatelle, since key positions for an overthrow had to be held by acceptable people. The use of camouflage became a moral duty. So Bonhoeffer took no offence, for instance, when his brother-in-law von Dohnanyi or General Oster kept in touch with men belonging to the SS. If there had to be a conspiracy, then they had to go into the lion's den and secure a foothold there. And if every rank and status in the country had been stripped of moral authority, if hope for an evolutionary change definitely remained unfulfilled, if the risk of bringing about war had now consciously been taken, if other nations were being ravished and the Jews liquidated, theological conclusions could no longer be morally refused. The consciences of the conspirators had to be set at rest, and this was Bonhoeffer's business.

An opposition that seriously sought to stop Hitler had to make sure of getting hold of the instruments of power. All political efforts at restraining Hitler, in the economic and legislative sphere as well as in foreign affairs, had failed; they now became of secondary importance compared with the task of gaining influence and key positions in the army. If the plot was a serious affair, it would in future have to be a military plot. For a man of Bonhoeffer's origins, convictions and circle of friends, it was not easy to arrive at this conclusion.

An extreme consequence of such military readiness became evident in the days when the German invasion of Holland, Belgium and France was in preparation. At that time Bonhoeffer first met Hans Oster, the central figure in the German military counter-espionage in Berlin, where a kind of secret office had been established by the conspiracy. Oster, who was to die with Bonhoeffer on 9 April 1945, was convinced that Hitler with his treacherous invasion of the Netherlands would irrevocably bring about ultimate disaster for Europe and Germany. Therefore he sacrificed his honour as an officer in order to obstruct wherever possible. Indeed, he informed the Dutch of the date of the planned attack! For this reason, Oster's name is hardly mentioned even today in ceremonies commemorating the opposition to Hitler. Bonhoeffer knew what Oster was doing and approved of it. He did not consider it treason, but on the contrary as a step taken in ultimate responsibility, appropriate in a situation where a presumptuous German had manoeuvred his country into an inevitable catastrophe, and where all those who were capable of action were suffering from a paralysis of conscience. So a patriot committed what in normal times is the action of a scoundrel. 'Treason' became true patriotism, and what was normally patriotism became, from the objective point of view, treason, whatever its subjective cause may have been. This officer saw the diabolical reversal of all values and acted entirely on his own. After what he had seen in Poland, where officers had witnessed powerlessly what, contrary to all international law, had been done to the Polish intelligentsia and the Jews, and had even had to take part in it, Oster did not want to help pave the way for new outrages in other countries in the name of Germany. And Bonhoeffer approved of the step he took.

It is difficult in normal times to realize the unhappy state of divided loyalties which these men experienced, or to understand why the most conscientious person had to accept disgrace. In such a situation, however, the Christian proves himself to be a Christian. Normally, treason implies a base disposition and it is engaged in for personal advantage and with the intention of harming one's country. The opposite holds good for these men.

During those months, Bonhoeffer worked at his *Ethics*, obviously no longer reluctant to theologize as in the United States, but now doing so with a new freedom and soberness. There we read:

> What is worse than doing evil is being evil. It is the worse for a liar to tell the truth than for a lover of truth to lie.[6]

3. PARTICIPATION

The third period, from the end of 1940 to 1943, is one of direct participation in underground political activities. Bonhoeffer's life now ran a fully determined course. To the outside world he remained a civilian and a theological expert of the Confessing Church. In the army he was a civilian employed by counterespionage to further their military aims. In reality he worked for the opposition, that is, for that group of the opposition whose centre was within counter-espionage. He travelled in order to contact Christians on the other side of the front-lines, and if possible to help them work out their ideas of peace. Finally, in 1942 in Sigtuna, he informed the British, through Bishop Bell, about plans for the overthrow of Hitler, submitted to them certain proposals, and vouched for the names involved. Thus he attempted to prevent an overthrow from outside the country. He also took part in efforts to save some Jews by getting them out of the country, again masquerading in this attempt as an agent of the *Abwehr*.

By now Bonhoeffer's life had become irrevocably tied to the vagaries of the war, far more than to the rear-guard actions of the Confessing Church. His loyalty to friends involved in the church struggle remained unchanged; but his most strenuous labours and attentions were devoted to his fellow-conspirators. In giving himself over to the logic of the conspiracy, he had to allow himself to be exploited as a man of the Church and of ecumenism. He could be made use of as an ecumenically known pastor who, by being trusted in Allied circles, made new contacts which were urgently needed by the conspiracy. He could not expect the leaders of the conspiracy to grant him special treatment because he was a clergyman. He had to share totally in camouflage and deceit. Not to have done so would have meant withholding full solidarity from those who, without enjoying any clerical privileges, had to act out their decisions with ever-increasing risk to their lives and reputations.

This state of affairs made him turn more than ever to his family and to old friends who were not very familiar with his life in Finkenwalde. The Finkenwalde group, for their part, were not allowed to enquire too much about his new activity. That kind of double life did not break him, but he clearly knew and felt that the responsible activist lives in ever-increasing loneliness. In a play he started to write in Tegel prison he makes the leading figure say:

What well-disposed man still utters contaminated words like

freedom, brotherliness, indeed Germany? He looks for them in the tranquillity of the sanctuary where only the humble and faithful may approach . . . Let us reverence the great ideals for a while in silence; let us learn for a time to do the right thing without words . . . Anyone who knows that his death is near is determined, but he is also silent. Without words, misunderstood and alone if need be, he does what is necessary and right, he makes his sacrifice.[7]

This double life was lived in the atmosphere of an increasingly frantic race: the race between the conspiracy, which aimed at abolishing the Gestapo, along with the system that made it possible, and the Gestapo, which aimed at getting all the secret services, including the military counter-espionage, under its control. On 5 April 1943, Bonhoeffer was arrested, not on account of his conspiratorial activities, but owing to the efforts of the Gestapo headquarters (the Reich Security Head Office) to prove that certain rules and agreements between them and the *Abwehr* had been broken; the intention was to gain control of the *Abwehr*. The Gestapo had no idea that, with this arrest, they had in fact made a direct hit at the heart of the conspiracy. This only became evident after the failure to assassinate Hitler on 20 July 1944.

During his internment in Tegel prison from April 1943 to the autumn of 1944, Bonhoeffer's main endeavour was to turn his interrogations into channels which made it possible for his friends outside to pursue their plans, and thus to protect them from suspicion. This was possible and successful until, following the events of 20 July 1944, the mass arrests and the discovery of the conspirators' files brought the truth to light, and all hope vanished.

4. EVALUATION

There is no unanimous evaluation of Bonhoeffer's political activity. Everything depends on whether it is viewed from within the framework of political resistance, or that of the Church. It sometimes seems as if discussion on it has not even started, if we consider, for instance, that the third period of Bonhoeffer's life, the political one, has been practically ignored in what has been written about him, and also in the reviews of the biography. This is especially so in Germany.

It is comparatively easy to evaluate Bonhoeffer's position within the political resistance movement, depending on one's perspective. Firstly, Bonhoeffer's activity in the resistance movement must not be overrated politically. He himself did not do so, but in his *Ethics* he indicates how much the method to be used by political conspiracy, and the timing, depend on an expert and practised judgement. Political ambition can hardly be imputed to him. Of course when he saw that practised political expertise threatened to become a pretext for not acting – 'The situation is far too complicated simply to act now!' – then he permitted himself robust judgements in the political sphere in order to prevent vital decisions from being shirked. His journey to Sweden in 1942 to meet Bell certainly assumed political importance of the first order; but there and then he did make it clear that he neither wished, nor was able, to be a politician. He knew perfectly well that his attempt to make contacts was only one among several, others of which were more expertly handled, and that his commission represented just one part of the whole structure.

Secondly, as regards planning for a future Germany and its constitutional forms, Bonhoeffer's share in the conspiracy was small. He has left us no draft for a future constitution. Admittedly he followed the wishes of the ecumenical movement and the Confessing Church in 1942, and encouraged and influenced the so-called Freiburg Group, consisting of Protestant experts in economics, law, politics and history, to work out plans; but personally he confined himself, within the framework of this enterprise, to working on the relationship between Church and State. For the future, he rather considered it his task to examine exhaustively the traditions of his Church and his Lutheran theology once the times were fit for such work. This, however, he looked upon as a far-reaching task.

Thirdly, from the point of view of the powers of intellectual penetration exhibited in the revolutionary movement, we must count Bonhoeffer among the foremost protagonists of the German political resistance. As we have seen, he immediately reflected on Oster's action and gave his thoughts expression, for example, in his analysis of the situation in his *Ethics*, and again, in a different form, in *Letters and Papers from Prison*, in the chapter 'After Ten Years'. What he said there about the breakdown of reasonableness, about the ethical rigorist, about the man of conscience and duty, and about private virtuousness in concrete historical situations like that of the Germans of that time, is still valid. This sober self-evaluation was not written *after* the event, but during one of the most promising phases of the resistance.[8] His words still speak to us when all the constitutional proposals of the resistance have been torn to shreds and forgotten. He wrote his analysis for his friends von Dohnanyi and Oster, to save them from being dazzled by an ideology, even a Christian one, and he did not let them forget that the common responsibility for Germany's shame and her survival in the family of nations was at stake:

> The ultimate question for a responsible man to ask is not how he is to extricate himself heroically from the affair, but how the coming generation is to live. It is only from this question, with its responsibility towards history, that fruitful solutions can come, even if for the time being they are very humiliating.[9]

Finally, if we consider to what degree Bonhoeffer shared in the conspiracy, his part is just as unquestionable as is his intellectual penetration. After a time of hesitation due to his profession and his former attitude, he gave himself completely to the common destiny without reserving for himself any exemption from the need for solidarity. Opportunist considerations were far removed from him, they never existed; in this regard Bonhoeffer belongs to the first rank of the conspirators.

It is far more difficult to evaluate Bonhoeffer's position as a Christian political conspirator within the framework of the

Christian Church. His is a unique case. He once applied the concept of being in a boundary situation to himself. What he meant in the first place was probably that through his position in the Church – he was not a parish minister and hence was not tied to a specific place – and through the special position of his family, with its political connections, he was free to take the course of action prompted by his own inner urges and the requests of his friends. In a letter of 18 November 1943, he wrote:

> I became certain that the duty had been laid on me to hold out in this situation with all its problems.[10]

Some people welcome this interpretation of Bonhoeffer's situation as a boundary one since it solves a delicate problem; others, however, see this boundary situation in its essentials as a pattern for an authentic Christian existence of the future, containing as it does elements that have to be integrated today. The word 'conspirator' is still a degrading term in German, and in normal and well-ordered times many people, including good Christians, hesitate to apply it to Bonhoeffer, let alone give it primary importance. There is no doubt that among Protestant churchmen Bonhoeffer is very nearly a unique case. Beside his stand only the names of Friedrich Justus Perels, the lawyer of the Confessing Church, and the theologians Eugen Gerstenmaier and Hans Schönfeld.

At this point it may help to describe the different stages of resistance to the Third Reich by the Churches. The first stage was something like passive resistance in the Churches, a nonconformism of the Confessing congregations and, beyond that, a withdrawal from social and political involvement into church activities. Now and then there were small public demonstrations, as for instance in front of the Dahlem church after Niemöller's arrest, or the sending of delegations to protest to certain government ministers.

The second stage was one of ideological resistance in public, effectively demonstrated in sermons or intimations from the pulpit by men like Niemöller, Wurm, and the Roman Catholic

Cardinal Graf von Galen – a far more dangerous and more responsible resistance. This resistance, however, did not draw up any plans for the political future of the community, nor did it strive for them. Here, not only nonconformism, but clear disobedience to certain laws was demanded. But there was no intention of shaping a new political structure; such a task was left to others.

Thirdly, there was the stage of being an accessory to preparations for a political revolt, which sometimes brought in church officials such as Asmussen, Dibelius, Lilje or Grüber, who were exposed to the greatest dangers if they did not impart their knowledge to the authorities. At this stage those involved, though politically passive themselves, were quite conscious of their share and sudden presence in political responsibility.

The fourth stage went even further by preparing for the post-revolt period, not, that is, preparing directly for a revolutionary overthrow by conspirators, but responsibly reflecting on the structure of a new community after the catastrophe which was certain to happen, either through a revolt, or through the defeat of the country. The most distinguished protagonist in this phase was Count von Moltke.

Finally there was the last stage, that of the fully-fledged conspiracy to which Bonhoeffer belonged, for which no more adequate name can be found. Participation in this conspiracy offered the greatest difficulty to somebody belonging to the Lutheran tradition, for this tradition provided the office of guardianship, but not the possibility of revolutionary interference as a conspirator. Luther did not exclude from justification opposition to a prince who infringes laws and constitution and thus has become a revolutionary himself. But Lutheranism forgot about and did not develop this possiblity, because for so long there had been no diabolically dictatorial government. In fact, previous governments had accepted Christian responsibilities, and hence a different state of affairs had not been imagined. So, in taking this fifth step, Bonhoeffer could expect no protection from the Church. There was no precedent for what had to be done.

In the circumstances then prevailing one could not wait to be drawn into a spontaneous uprising, into open revolutionary out-break, and then suddenly be forced to take one side or another without having responsibly prepared for it. There was no such spontaneous rising in Germany, nor was it expected by those opposed to Hitler. So Bonhoeffer had to commit himself, in the strictest sense, to a carefully prepared and responsibly planned conspiracy entailing so much equivocation that a masquerade had to be carried on and perfected, better if possible than that perpetrated by the enemy. It was no longer an opposition such as might have been possible in an earlier stage of the developing dictatorship; it was now the kind of conspiracy which is war-ranted only when the people who are called on to bear responsi-bility in the various branches of life have grown dumb, and when tyranny wielded in the name of those it rules has stained that name with blood in the face of all the world. Now, and only now, the time had come for this form of political struggle. A dangerous form indeed, risking the upheaval of the whole body politic during a war. For that reason it was only to be justified when it promised success and when all attempts had been made to safeguard it from outside. Only now was the Christian asked, on moral grounds, to take part in the conspiracy.

Bonhoeffer did not expect his Church publicly to uphold him and put him on the intercession lists of the various congregations. He forsook the support of a protective commonly held ethics, at a time when perhaps he needed it most. He had to accept general condemnation and leave his justification to God alone. As early as 1932, Bonhoeffer said in a sermon – and he did not know how prophetic his words were – that the time might come again when martyrdom would be called for,

> but this blood . . . will not be so innocent and clear as that of the first who testified. On our blood a great guilt would lie: that of the useless servant who is cast into the outer darkness.[11]

5. BONHOEFFER'S OWN INTERPRETATION

What did Bonhoeffer himself say about his step? Did he justify it? I should like to stress that he did *not* justify it, but he was ready to explain and answer for it. He put hardly anything about it on paper, for obvious historical as well as inner and theological reasons.

Some passages in his letters indicate beyond all doubt that he had come to terms with his decisions and their consequences. Thus he wrote at Christmas 1943 from his prison cell:

> Now I want to assure you that I haven't for a moment regretted coming back in 1939 – nor any of the consequences, either. I knew quite well what I was doing, and I acted with a clear conscience . . . And I regard my being kept here . . . as being involved in Germany's fate . . . I don't look back on the past and accept the present reproachfully.[12]

But he could not deal directly with the conspiracy in his writings, either biographically or theologically. In the first place it was too dangerous to provide the enemy with any written material giving clues. Who could possibly have anything lying around which dealt with the subject of the conspiracy? It would not only have been reckless, it would have proved an entire lack of seriousness. Furthermore, it just was not his way, nor the way of the other conspirators, to accompany and secure their enterprise in advance by apologetic self-justification. In any case, was there a platform where such a justification could be pronounced? The Churches were no longer competent, as they had neither realized the extent of the injustice, nor escaped their own shame. The theologians had not reflected on the crisis of ethics. The German public had ignored the fact that all the rules of war had been broken. Ecumenism also was blind to the guilt in which Christian nations had involved themselves, by refusing, for example, entry to Jewish refugees. None of them offered any platform for justification. Even today it is embarrassing to feel that Christians consciously or subconsciously expect Bonhoeffer to justify his activities as a conspirator. Should it not be the other way round?

Certainly Bonhoeffer did not think of his action as the best possible, but only as a very belated answer to what had been left undone at an earlier stage. We have his notes about the interrogations, which brutally reveal the terrible necessity of masquerading. He did not destroy these notes, but specially asked for them to be preserved. He who wants to justify himself destroys such things. But Bonhoeffer wished to bear responsibility for himself and his time, leaving the justification to God.

Bonhoeffer's *Ethics* does not contain any direct 'theology of revolution' either. In fact there are quite conservative passages, as when he says:

According to Holy Scripture, there is no right to revolution.[13]

This passage, however, goes on in a way which he has developed elsewhere too:

but there is a responsibility of every individual for preserving the purity of his office and mission in the *polis* . . . No one, not even government itself, can deprive him of this responsibility or forbid him to discharge it, for it is an integral part of his life in sanctification.[14]

This last sentence, written in the early forties, says a great deal, indirectly, about Bonhoeffer's own share in the conspiracy. Here belongs the chapter on 'What is Meant by "Telling the Truth"?' which was written at the time of his interrogations. It does not explain ethics as an alternative choice between black and white, that is as an ethics of obedience or revolution, but it shows that responsibility before God and men is a highly complex historical process. Particularly important here is the chapter on the structure of responsible and representative action, and the position of him who bears responsibility to laws and principles, or rather to man beloved in the name of Jesus Christ.

In the course of historical life there comes a point where the exact observance of the formal law of a state ... suddenly finds itself in violent conflict with the ineluctable necessities of the lives of men; at this point responsible and pertinent action leaves behind it the domain of principle and convention, the domain of the normal and regular, and is confronted by the extraordinary situation of ultimate necessities, a situation which no law can control ... these necessities ... cannot ... be governed by any law or themselves constitute a law ...

The extraordinary necessity appeals to the freedom of the men who are responsible. There is now no law behind which the responsible man can seek cover ... In this situation there can only be a complete renunciation of every law, together with the knowledge that here one must make one's decision as a free venture, together also with the open admission that here the law is being infringed and violated ... Precisely in this breaking of the law the validity of the law is acknowledged ...

If any man tries to escape guilt in responsibility he detaches himself from the ultimate reality of human existence, and what is more he cuts himself off from the redeeming mystery of Christ's bearing guilt without sin and he has no share in the divine justification which lies upon this event. He sets his own personal innocence above his responsibility for men, and he is blind to the more irredeemable guilt which he incurs precisely in this.[15]

Finally, the letters and papers from prison have to be interpreted as an attempt – perhaps an unconscious attempt – to reflect on, and express, the boundary situation as the pattern for a future way of being a Christian.

Read in the light of Bonhoeffer's return from America and his joining of the conspiracy, his *Cost of Discipleship* and *Life Together* appear almost like the private confessions of a Christian. The Church which he had once so enthusiastically discovered had meanwhile in her actions and her utterances become guilty of sterility – whereas his friends and family, whom he had once criticized for their humanism and liberalism, and their only marginal interest in the Church, were doing what had to be done. It was this situation which had to be pondered on and expressed afresh so that the true message of Jesus Christ would come alive, convincing these secular and worldly men and women that it was they who were meant and addressed by it. For this reason, Bonhoeffer in his prison cell set to work to conceive his theology once again.

SIX

Authentic Theology

In his *Letters and Papers from Prison* we now reach the point in
Bonhoeffer's life and thought where, after experiencing a
'disciplina pietatis' and a sense of 'worldly responsibility', he
raises the question about an authentic theology more intensely
than ever before. The slogans that are now current everywhere –
non-religious interpretation, religionless Christianity, world
come of age, arcane discipline, Jesus the man for others, the
Church for others – all of these are concerned in the fullest sense
with theology, and not with a transformation of theology into
philosophy and anthropology.

In the *Union Seminary Quarterly Review* the Swiss Henry
Mottu once pointed out how, at the end, Bonhoeffer's theology
is dominated by, and remains in a continual discussion with,
Feuerbach's unanswered question about the truth and the reality
of talking about God.[1] We actually find in Bonhoeffer's first
Berlin lecture of 1931 the following sentence: 'Feuerbach put two
questions to theology which remained unanswered: 1. about
the *truth* of her proposition, 2. about their relevance to real
life.'[2]

We may rightly understand Bonhoeffer's life and actions as a
struggle with these questions of Feuerbach. But in total contrast
to Feuerbach, whose questions implied the denial of any authenticity and truth in the matter of faith, Bonhoeffer's concern was
to show with regard to the very same questions the authenticity
of the Christian kerygma. As we know, Barth also took up
Feuerbach's questions, but his answers were more cautious, and
his treatment of the matter unmistakably Trinitarian as, for example, in his essay *The Humanity of God*. Moreover, he had the
time to deal with it systematically. Bonhoeffer risked more,
throwing himself almost exclusively on to Christology. He

stepped nearer, dangerously nearer, the theological abyss and set more in motion than either Barth or Feuerbach ever did. But I would not say, as some people do, that he has taken us into the abyss.

I. BACKGROUND

What did Bonhoeffer really say when in Tegel prison, in 1944, he once again began to formulate his understanding of theology? His last thoughts, as far as they are preserved, are contained in a four-page outline which he sent me from his prison cell in August 1944. It is a summary of the theological reflection in the letters of his last months and the structure for a book which he planned to write.[3] He probably worked at the manuscript during the next few months, first in Tegel, and then in the Gestapo prison; but it is lost. We have nothing but these last scanty clues. But they do say something if we consider who said them, to whom he said them, and when he said them.

Who wrote these brief lines? That man of the Church, that preacher, that man of political action we have spoken about – in other words, a man who had in no way lost his certainty, but who had always been opposed to apologetics. A man who in Tegel prison stressed that he understood himself not as breaking with his past, but as developing in an unbroken continuity. He saw himself as the heir of a highly civilized European middle class which he affirmed and loved. And now, at the end, the thought was well-nigh unbearable to him that a century of so-called secularization, of an intellectual attitude opposed to the Church, should lie beyond the reach of God and Christ. In his prison letters he therefore reformulated his old basic question: 'Who is Christ for us today?' He did not ask this question anxiously, even then, nor did he ask: 'How may faith survive today?' This very question would have been for him an admission of defeat, which he never considered. Neither did he ask: 'What does modern man need?' His faith in the majesty of Christ did not allow such a question. He asked positively, presupposing

Christ as present. He did not start a discussion on the necessity and usefulness of this presence, but he discussed the fact of this presence, and who Christ is for us today. 'Us' – that is, he himself, as a double heir of, and doubly responsible for, the historical Church to which he belonged and the middle-class world from which he came. In this context, he asked about the truth and the reality of faith, like Feuerbach, and yet in quite a different way. Feuerbach by his questions had already rejected both; Bonhoeffer by his very questions presupposed faith. He took Feuerbach's questions seriously, and insisted that an answer should be given by believers about the truth and reality of their faith. But he did not ask *whether* the faith is true and real, but *how* it is so, and *who* may prove it as such, where, and in what circumstances. He did not ask these questions as one who destroys, but as one who renews.

In what situation did he write? Bonhoeffer wrote after having experienced that the great traditional words of his Church had become hollow, emptied of their power. He wrote during a period in the history of his Church which was different from ours, when the danger was not so much one of being cheaply familiar with the world, but rather one of being removed from the world and pushed into a ghetto. The diastasis of the Church and the world was overwhelming; any solidarity between them had either been brought about the wrong way, or had vanished altogether. When he wrote these letters, Bonhoeffer thought that for a long time to come the Church had forfeited all her established privileges and generally recognized corporate rights (here he was mistaken as far as Germany was concerned), and, in view of that situation, the form and content of the message had to be pondered afresh. This implies, of course, that a Church which is firmly established in her privileged position may not be wholly fit to share Bonhoeffer's thoughts. He had received new stimulus from meeting the conspirators, most of whom just could not settle back into the structures provided by the existing Church. Other stimuli were provided by an intense reading, in his prison cell, of nineteenth-century literature and philosophy, and especially fruitful was the discovery of Dilthey. Thus Bonhoeffer wrote:

> I feel obliged to tackle these questions as one who, although a 'modern' theologian, is still aware of the debt that he owes to liberal theology. There will not be many of the younger men in whom these two trends are combined.[4]

He did not write, then, in a situation like that in which he wrote *The Cost of Discipleship*; for him, 'modern' means what Barth's theology had discovered, and brought to predominance, a theology of the Church. He does not wish to assert this theology as an exclusive alternative to the problems of the nineteenth century, rather he wishes to take it up from the beginning again.

To whom did he write? Bonhoeffer did not send the letters and the outline of his manuscript to the world at large, nor even to his Church; he shared his thoughts with a theological friend in the Confessing Church. Certainly, he had planned a book which one day might open a responsible discussion with many people. But what we have was addressed to a very limited circle of people who understood his intentions.

This means that it was not his intention to convince the world that it was of age and religionless; he did not envisage such a vast programme. In a far more modest way he wished to prepare a few ministers for a new situation in their Church, when the phenomena of religionlessness and the loss of privileges would have to be faced. He wanted his Church to see, in quite a new way, that there was a process of emancipation going on around her, and he wanted to enable her to grasp Christ as the Lord of this process. This was a modest undertaking, yet one which has become revolutionary. But Bonhoeffer really did not debate with the world, or with statisticians, about whether or not they were able to find enough people of age, and enough religionless ones; he wrote to a friend: Look, this is what our faith is like if we have accepted this or that in the historical processes which we experience, no matter who we may have become aware of them through, Feuerbach, Dilthey, or Nietzsche. As a pastor, he wished to help us, and the Church, in this context, to expect new insights from the old Gospel in trust and courage, and to be ready to risk something for this. Thus we read in the covering letter to his friend:

I'm enclosing the outline of a book . . . I hope I shall be given the peace and strength to finish it. The Church must come out of its stagnation. We must move out again into the open air of intellectual discussion with the world, and risk saying controversial things, if we are to get down to the serious problems of life . . . How very useful your help would be! But even if we are prevented from clarifying our minds by talking things over, we can still pray, and it is only in the spirit of prayer that any such work can be begun and carried through.[5]

Ten days later he wrote, 'I'm finding the work so fascinating',[6] implying that its spell was carrying him through the days of the failure of the conspiracy, with their new arrests and executions going on around him. What he was writing then did not involve a struggle against Hitler. Hitler was no longer worthy to be dealt with theologically. It was the future task of the Church which entirely engaged Bonhoeffer's attention: 'I hope it may be of some help for the Church's future.'[7] These are the last words of the outline of the book, clearly indicating once again to whom it is addressed.

This 'Outline' promised three chapters: 1. A Stocktaking of Christianity, 2. The Real Meaning of Christian Faith, 3. Conclusions. Bonhoeffer's first intention was to make us see what characterizes and conditions Western Christianity, and with it the Protestant Church today. Sometimes he briefly referred to subjects mentioned earlier in his letters. In the second chapter he followed this up by interpreting the signs of faith, again in a rather disproportionate way, on the basis of subjects dealt with (or not dealt with) before. Thirdly, he was concerned with problems of the new form the Church and the ministry were going to take, and not just with questions of interpretation, as Ebeling claimed in his famous essay on Bonhoeffer.[8]

2. STOCKTAKING

Apparently it is not easy to see things clearly. Vested interests and doctrinal premises make the Church clumsy, too clumsy to perceive the ongoing historical processes around her and within her; they make her prone to relate herself and her cause to the wrong address, thus finally misunderstanding and misinterpreting herself to such a degree that she loses her genuine identity. For Bonhoeffer this situation had become so critical that he did not start his 'Outline' with Christology, as elsewhere, but with an analysis of the present time. He no longer shied away from establishing other 'points of departure', which had become anathema in the Confessing Church since Karl Barth, who had seen in this the great danger of admitting another source of revelation. But Bonhoeffer obviously did not see this as a problem now, as if the source of proclamation could be prejudiced by such an analysis of the situation. On the contrary, just because he was concerned with the proclamation, his interest focused on the proclaimer and the person addressed. He had once mentioned this, in a letter to myself, with reference to preaching: 'One has to live for some time in a community to understand how Christ is "formed" in it (Galatians 4:19).'[9] *Living with others* is the first presupposition for an appropriate, non-ideological knowledge. And that now meant: to think, experience, long for, act, along with the people of our present history; and for this, so he thought, his commitment to Christ set him free. Thus we now recognize in Bonhoeffer a new freedom to see and dare to judge in the fields of secular history, spiritual history and phenomenology. Why should faith prevent our eyes from being opened to see what there is, what there will be and what will pass away? On the contrary, faith sharpens curiosity in its historical processes, and within them Christianity.

Bonhoeffer first turned his attention to the process of *coming of age* in Western intellectual history. In his 'Outline' he only indicated what he had said earlier at greater length, beginning with the letter of 8 June 1944. All the same, the discovery of personal responsibility took pride of place here. He characterized the modern world as passing through 'a process of coming of age', which is not the same as a 'process of secularization' or a 'struggle for autonomy'. Earlier, he had used these terms too. But after he had read Dilthey in the summer of 1944, the concept of maturity with which he was already familiar from Kant prevailed, replacing the others almost entirely.

Maturity is a description for a historical development in the Western world which sweeps through all philosophy, natural sciences, law, and even religion. Bonhoeffer was not concerned with statistics, but, drawing an analogy with the coming of age in physical growth and legal status of the twenty-one-year-old, he described how men, groups and epochs become responsible for themselves. He reminded us how people gradually fight free of the heterogenous tutelage which keeps them, like children, in bondage. By 'maturity' he meant something which was a right due to everybody, along with all other human rights, a right which, if withheld from men, was bound to do harm not only to those from whom it was withheld but also to those who withheld it.

For two hundred years the Churches have understood this right as a threat to their role as guardians and mediators, and they have opposed it polemically as wicked secularization and a great apostasy from God. Bonhoeffer now wanted and felt bound to acknowledge this right as a great good, for the sake of God and Christ. The 'heteronomy' of our relation to Christ remains, of course, as part of our maturity; but he did not see it as a tutelage to keep man in bondage. The crucified Christ is in fact a guarantee of our being of age in the sense of personal responsibility. Christ does not destroy but releases this.

Bonhoeffer's concept of being of age as the key and sign of our time has proved so fascinating that some took it up too hastily and uncritically; others rejected it equally hastily without examining it, suspecting it as a heritage of the Enlightenment. The Americans saw it as a reaffirmation of their optimistic belief in progress, a view which was only possible where there was ignorance of Bonhoeffer the theologian and heir of the Reformation who never forgot the '*cor corvum in se*'. In fact, Bonhoeffer developed this very part of the 'Outline' in a way which hardly allows of any optimistic belief in progress. For there he explained in a little more detail how man, including man come of age, is his own greatest enemy and how, by trying to satisfy his desire for security and independence with the help of organizations, he bars his own way to maturity. This realistic, sober self-knowledge of man does not, however, invalidate an acknowledgement of his maturity. It stresses the demand for it, laying upon Christians the responsibility, out of the strength of their faith, for helping new generations, groups or individuals to become themselves, and the responsibility for preventing them from being kept in dependence.

In outgrowing the times of tutelage, man also shakes off his oldest guardians, religion and its functionaries. So the second paragraph in this chapter was devoted to *religionlessness*. For the sciences, the disappearance of tutelage meant that they turned away from 'God as a working hypothesis' and freely developed the fields of philosophy and natural sciences according to their own laws. Here Bonhoeffer was concerned with correcting the theological error of describing any talk of God as 'filling the gap' where scientific knowledge is at an end and human needs seek for an answer.

By 'religion' Bonhoeffer understood a complex of quite definite ideas and views about God which are untenable when tested by the actual facts as well as by biblical faith. God as a working hypothesis and a stop-gap has indeed lost his truth and reality, and in this sense we live in a religionless age. Here again Bonhoeffer did not enumerate the amount of still existing and perhaps even newly revived need of man for 'religion'. There is still a considerable amount of that touching the margins of people's lives. But that which in fact organizes the world today, plans it, runs it, explains it, that which answers for what is real and sustains it politically, economically, scientifically, is not religion. In this sense, its time has irrevocably gone. But for Bonhoeffer that never meant that the time of Christ had gone.

This analysis of our present time dealt in the next section with the way in which the Protestant Church had reacted to this upheaval in her view of the world and her ideas, whether by pietism, by orthodoxy, or by the more recent form of the Confessing Church. According to Bonhoeffer, she had always reacted by trying to secure a religious sphere over against the world, and from within the shelter of this sphere, she had attempted to prove that she was indispensable. But the Church, by her very anxiety to preserve a special, unassailable place for herself, had become a watchdog of religion, an institution catering for the marginal problems of man, privileged, yes, but shut away from the world. As such a keeper of religion she was finished. She asserts her necessity but cannot realize it, therefore she lingers on in apologetics and self-defence. So Bonhoeffer concluded: 'The decisive factor: The Church on the defensive. No taking risks for others.'[10]

3. THE MEANING OF THE CHRISTIAN FAITH

From a theological point of view, the second chapter is the most exciting one. Having dispatched Christianity as a religion, Bonhoeffer now tried to put it on a new foundation by, (a) dealing with the question of God in relation to the world, (b) establishing this question as a Christological one, (c) announcing the non-religious interpretation of biblical concepts, (d) raising the question of worship, and (e) stressing the honesty of mature faith. It becomes immediately evident from these themes that Bonhoeffer's religionlessness never meant the end of faith in God, but only the end of a certain prevailing kind of faith in God; and what he was really concerned with during his imprisonment was the fresh authenticity of the Gospel in changed circumstances, of which the Church so far had not taken account. Long-cherished ideas had to be given up; but only in order to liberate man to know the Gospel more truly, and at the same time help him to become aware of his own epoch. Only then would the Church be able to address man, to preach to him, and to communicate with him.

In the first paragraph Bonhoeffer indicated a great theme with one single phrase: *God and the World*. After showing that the development towards maturity and religionlessness had pushed faith in God out of the world, and into a ghetto, he now wished to explain that in reality God and the world are related to each other indispensably, but that unfortunately faith in God has been falsified by a static way of thinking in two compartments. Here Bonhoeffer apparently wanted to elucidate what he had mentioned earlier, namely that everything we can responsibly know or say of God aims at the heart of this life and its actual responsibilities, and not in the first place at the dark unenlightened recesses of life.

Strictly speaking, Bonhoeffer's subject here is not 'God and the World' but 'Worldliness and God'. This meant that he did not dream of identifying God and the world, or relinquishing eschatology and transcendence. On the contrary, he wanted to rediscover genuine transcendence by drawing it down from its aloofness. God and the world are not one and the same thing, but God and worldliness belong together as truly as God is God. He had dealt with this more fully in his *Ethics* and previous letters.

Benjamin Reist has convincingly argued that *Ethics* and the letters from prison belong together in overcoming the static way of thinking in two separated realms, and that Bonhoeffer has brought the talk about God into the middle of the world and thus placed the Church in her proper context:

> The real concept of the secular, then – not the 'secularism', that has so often given the term its negative connotation – has to do with the fact that that which is Christian can be found only in the world.[11]

And Bonhoeffer says in his *Ethics*:

> It is now essential to the real concept of the secular that it shall always be seen in the movement of being accepted and becoming accepted by God in Christ. Just as in Christ the reality of God entered into the reality of the world, so, too, is that which is Christian to be found only in that which is of the world, the

'supernatural' only in the natural, the holy only in the profane, and the revelational only in the rational. The unity of the reality of God and of the world, which has been accomplished in Christ, is repeated, or, more exactly, is realized, ever afresh in the life of men. And yet what is Christian is not identical with what is of the world. The natural is not identical with the supernatural or the revelational with the rational. But between the two there is in each case a unity which derives solely from the reality of Christ, that is to say solely from faith in this ultimate reality. This unity is seen in the way in which the secular and the Christian elements prevent one another from assuming any kind of static independence in their mutual relations. They adopt a polemical attitude towards each other and bear witness precisely in this to their shared reality and to their unity in the reality which is in Christ . . .

Luther was protesting against a Christianity which was striving for independence and detaching itself from the reality in Christ. He protested with the help of the secular and in the name of a better Christianity. So, too, today, when Christianity is employed as a polemical weapon against the secular, this must be done in the name of a better secularity and above all it must not lead back to a static predominance of the spiritual sphere as an end in itself. It is only in this sense, as a polemical unity, that Luther's doctrine of the two kingdoms is to be accepted, and it was no doubt in this sense that it was originally intended.[12]

But who is this God? With this question the second paragraph went to the very heart of Bonhoeffer's theology. The answer is Christological, in the sense of a *theologia crucis*. Barth once pointed out the dangers involved in developing Christology only, and expressly kept to the Trinitarian equilibrium of theology. We have to remember, however, that what Bonhoeffer wanted to concentrate on in his Christology was theology. In this section we have to take great care to note how Bonhoeffer kept questions and answers together. Every Christological sentence in this paragraph begins quite clearly with the question of our relation to

God: 'Who is God?'; 'That is not a genuine experience of *God*'; 'Our relation to God is not . . .'; 'God in human form.' In other words, his Christology is not concerned to make transcendence imminent, but to give it a fresh actuality.

The experience of God certainly takes place in meeting Christ, the Incarnate, Crucified and Risen One who is there for others. At this point Bonhoeffer answered Feuerbach's question about the truth and reality of theology. Feuerbach's dissolution of theology into anthropology had unmasked theology as an expression of the promise to fulfil men's this-worldly desires in a world beyond, and to relieve their needs. Bonhoeffer took this up but changed it around. He accepted Feuerbach's criticisms of religion; but for him, the Christian experience of God through the biblical Christ says exactly the opposite: man does not delegate himself to an almighty God, but God in weakness delegates himself to man. For Bonhoeffer, the substance of faith is not man existing for a despotic God, but the experience that a total transformation of human existence is given in the fact that Jesus is there for others.

Feuerbach endeavoured, by making 'the candidates of the here-after into students of this world', to change them into atheists; but Bonhoeffer, with the same phrase, wanted to make them into Christians. In this sense he took up Feuerbach, in the first stanza of his famous poem 'Christians and Unbelievers', saying with him:

> Men go to God when they are sore bestead,
> Pray to him for succour, for his peace, for bread,
> For mercy for them sick, sinning, or dead;
> All men do so, Christian and unbelieving.

This is the Feuerbach stanza. Bonhoeffer answered:

> Men go to God when he is sore bestead,
> Find him poor and scorned, without shelter or bread,
> Whelmed under weight of the wicked, the weak, the dead;
> Christians stand by God in his hour of grieving.[13]

Men seek the *deus ex machina*, the powerful almighty; for Bonhoeffer, as for Feuerbach, that is a 'partial extension of the world', everybody wants it, it does not make Christians. And this is what Bonhoeffer calls 'religious'; its end is drawing near. But Jesus' freedom from self, his concern for others, 'maintained till death, that is the ground of his omnipotence, omniscience, and omnipresence. Faith is participation in this being of Jesus.'[14] That points to the way in which Bonhoeffer answered his life's question, 'Who Christ really is for us today', and with it, the question about God. And in this connection he formulated the apparently simple and yet so meaningful and new title for Christ: Jesus the man for others. That is Christ the Crucified and Risen One; in him transcendence takes place, and the experience of God.

Only now, after analysing the world (a development towards release from tutelage also implies the decline of religion and certain images of God); after analysing the Church (her attempts to secure a safe place absorb the Church in self-defence); after stating the biblical God's relatedness to the world, and the Christological reversal of an experience of God such as man naturally longs for – only after all this does the subject follow which has been most hotly debated: *the non-religious interpretation of biblical concepts*. In the 'Outline' he does not enlarge on it but only describes it as the consequence of the starting-point in his theological Christology. Whoever proclaims Christ through interpreting his 'being for others' must now try to read the sources of this formula in the Bible and doctrine without those inherited presuppositions and ideas and word-structures which hitherto seemed obligatory, but which have turned those sources into a petrified religion. Bonhoeffer here dealt with 'creation, fall, atonement, repentance, faith, the new life, the last things'.

In his correspondence with me Bonhoeffer had defined religious interpretation in two directions: metaphysical and individualistic. By this he meant, on the one hand, Greek ontic or Thomistic metaphysics and the language moulded dogmatically by it; that is, the language cut out and tailored for faith since the early ages. On the other hand, he meant the expectation of salvation which since Luther had become one-sided on the basis of an absolutized doctrine of justification, an expectation which had allowed vast biblical concepts like 'the Kingdom' to wither away. Non-religious interpretation thus claimed to grasp, and to declare, the contents of the Gospel in such a way that it was able to form a new synthesis with fresh metaphysics, which meant the language and ideas of our modern world; and, in freeing itself from the post-Reformation narrowness, opened up its relation to the whole reality of our world. Hence he thought of an interpretation which liberates, encourages, directs and renews responsibility for the realities of the world. It is not by erecting new power-structures in sermon and dogma, and thus awakening or cementing new expectations of a *deus ex machina*, but by revealing the lordship of the Crucified One, of Jesus carrying his cross, a lordship which strangely disqualified all other lordships, that man will be set free from tutelage. Such an interpretation rescues the Gospel from its provincialism; it no longer allows God to be looked upon as an unapproachable despot to whom man must be sacrificed (Feuerbach), but points to God sacrificing himself, so that man may live – a reversal of Feuerbach's description of Christianity.

The token [sign] of the non-religious God is actually his weakness, not his exploitation of my weakness.[15]

We must be clear that Bonhoeffer made a difference between his negative concept of 'religion', and life lived in faith. But how do we grasp his 'Jesus for others'? What about the 'religious' life of a congregation – liturgy, prayer and assembly? I asked Bonhoeffer about it, and he immediately felt that in this matter his case had to stand the test. But unfortunately at this point he failed to give us any guidance. We only read in the fourth paragraph of the second chapter: 'Cultus. (Details to follow later, in particular on cultus and "religion".)'[16] But he knew that it needed a special chapter.

Although we do not have more, it is clear that Bonhoeffer never envisaged that the identity of the Christian would be destroyed by solidarity with worldly men and duties; that it would be dissolved by the worldly non-religious interpretation.

On the contrary, he believed that meeting 'the Jesus for others' must be disciplined through and strengthened in worship and prayer. In earlier letters he once spoke very positively of 'genuine worship'. He knew all too well that he who is nothing has nothing to say. He who is nothing himself is not capable of any solidarity worth speaking of. You have to become something, you have to keep on being something, and becoming and being something happens to people meeting the Word, meeting the brothers, and sharing comfort and praise with them.

At this point Bonhoeffer introduced a concept which was first ignored and later aroused suspicion: 'arcane discipline'.[17] He may not have been cautious enough in ignoring the implicit undertone of the mystery religions in this concept, the secretiveness of a Gnostic elite, but what interested him was the fact that for the Christian there had always been situations, and there was one now, where the public interpretation by words deafens men and prevents them hearing the true Gospel, thus making them immune to it for a long time. This may be brought about by an experience of wrong-doing (an experience like that which Christians in Germany underwent in their treatment of the Jews). It may also result from words being used up and worn out, because of the complete divergence between the preaching and the actual nature of the Church, which has cried out so blatantly that all talk loses its authenticity.

Finally, Bonhoeffer turns to the problem of the honesty with which the faith of a *theologia crucis* is expressed. Honesty, however, is a way of authenticity. Honesty and authenticity flourish where a mature Christian speaks himself, where he no longer entrenches himself behind tradition, behind creeds or synods. Christian education and theological studies today produce a certain hesitation about saying in one's own words what one stands for. Here we have to mention Bonhoeffer's discovery that words have their time, their speaker and their hearer, and thus their fixed place and meaning, a time when and a place where they become authentic. This is a matter of freeing Christian faith from any ideology, as is most clearly and effectively expressed in

Bonhoeffer's essay 'What is Meant by "Telling the Truth"?' Mottu suggests another title: 'The essay might have been called: What we have to do to get away from the illusory and unrelated eternal truth in order to find the real, genuine truth.'[18]

4. CONSEQUENCES FOR THE CHURCH

The third chapter of the 'Outline' is entirely devoted to the problem of the form of the Church. Bonhoeffer submits proposals for its existence in a non-religious world, a world come of age. In the second chapter a non-religious interpretation was discussed within the German tradition, whereas now a religionless Christianity is being described – the phrase which in the English-speaking world is considered *the* characteristic cue of Bonhoeffer's theology. Bonhoeffer's proposals have been written down somewhat loosely and hurriedly; all the same, it is as clear as can be that we are not to think of a religionless Christianity as a churchless Christianity. For *the* theme of this final chapter is the Church and her transformation.

The first sentence contains the ecclesiological formula which exactly corresponds to the Christological one in the second chapter, and which in 1968 became the slogan of the World Council of Churches Assembly at Uppsala: 'The Church is the Church only when it exists for others.'[19] One is sometimes tempted to eradicate the word 'only' in view of the signs of dissolution, and the minimalism and purely functional quality of the Church as some people conceive it today. When Bonhoeffer coined the phrases the situation was different; the danger of dissolution did not consist in accommodation to the world, but in the Gospel being pushed into a ghetto. But there is a secret about the word 'only', namely, that the Church retains her character as the community of Christ only if she remains true to him in her ways and demands nothing for herself.

Religionless Christianity, then, is represented by a Church which more or less knows how to solve her problem of identity and identification under this law of Christ: being herself in not wanting anything for herself. Thus Bonhoeffer reduces his ecclesiology to something demanding the simplest possible qualification, but it is an ecclesiology which has only been achieved after a long journey involving his own life, the history of the Church and the times, and after intense theological thought. The authenticity of the cause, its truth and its reality are contained in this formula 'Church for others', in such a convincing way that others may be drawn into this process of authenticity, and authenticity itself remains grounded in the gift of God.

Bonhoeffer continued by making some practical proposals for the Church and her offices in a religionless era. Some are convincing, others seem naïve today, and even one-sided. Sometimes the proposals in their cryptic form are difficult to connect. The first proposal says that the inherited privileged corporate rights of the Church are to be done away with – the task of the Church can hardly be reconciled with her endeavour to safeguard herself by possessions and landed properties. Bonhoeffer himself never quite saw his profession within the framework of those 'duties and rights of the clergy' which are so highly respected in Germany. He may have been too self-reliant and careless, as only an aristocrat can afford to be. All the same, the separation of the offices of pastor and preacher is being discussed today, and there are attempts in Germany to functionalize the ministry in ways which may be an interpretation of what Bonhoeffer indicated. The first duty of the Church shall not consist in presenting a public cultus. She must not try to play the preceptor, but 'must share in the secular problems of ordinary human life'.[20] This has been taken up by some well-known memoranda of the Evangelical Church in Germany.

The task of the Church in a non-religious era should be to express the being of Christ in the centre of life, not on its margins. Here Bonhoeffer enumerated highly sensible, normal demands which have nothing mysterious and special about them. They remind us of St Paul's lists of virtues, which describe Christian life in very normal and human terms, and which do not care for any *proprium*. We remember St Paul's 'reasonable service'

(Romans 12:1). Here things are mentioned which purify and sustain life together. The list should always be examined and adapted to the times. The list of virtues is followed by a reference to the 'example'. Authenticity demands interest in the speaking and acting word. Bonhoeffer wanted to rediscover St Paul's candour in being, and to revise the Reformers' dislike of it: 'It is not abstract argument, but example, that gives its [the Church's] word emphasis and power.'[21] For this, Bonhoeffer himself became the martyr.

In conclusion, Bonhoeffer mentioned the need for revising the Apostles' Creed, apologetics, training for the ministry, and the pattern of clerical life. What was the reason for naming all these together? Perhaps Bonhoeffer thought that all these things which need revision (Creed, apologetics, ministry) act as barriers and road-blocks in their present form. They are ancient dogmatic fixations of the Church acting as religion; the Church keeps and protects them and thus allows the preaching of the freedom of the Gospel to be obscured. Thus, the discovery of the 'Church for others' and 'Jesus for others' is also thwarted. Bonhoeffer well knew how provisional his remarks were:

All this is very crude and condensed, but there are certain things that I'm anxious to say simply and clearly – things that we so often like to shirk.

Sometimes I'm quite shocked at what I say, especially in the first part, which is mainly critical; and so I'm looking forward to getting to the more constructive part.[22]

Bonhoeffer did not live to write 'the more constructive part'; he died it. Perhaps, in view of our present situation, his far too unsophisticated remarks are less important than the action of his life, his participation in the name of the Crucified One. By that, more than by anything else, we are called upon to recognize and develop, without 'religion', the gift of these new beginnings.

SEVEN

Modern Martyrdom

During the last century a lonely Protestant pastor, Michael Baumgarten (1812–89), was expelled from his pulpit and his chair as Professor of Old Testament in Rostock by the Lutheran authorities of Mecklenburg. He had discovered more in the Bible about the revolution of humanity than the Church sanctioned. He once wrote these words:

> There are times in which lectures and publications no longer suffice to communicate the necessary truth. At such times the deeds and sufferings of the saints must create a new alphabet in order to reveal again the secret of the truth.[1]

On 19 June 1932, Dietrich Bonhoeffer said in a sermon in the Kaiser-Wilhelm Memorial Church in Berlin:

> We must not be surprised if once again times return for our Church when the blood of martyrs will be required. But even if we have the courage and faith to spill it, this blood will not be as innocent or as clear as that of the first martyrs. Much of our own guilt will lie in our blood. The guilt of the useless servant who is thrown into the darkness.[2]

Such times did indeed come in Germany, when Protestants and Catholics surprisingly took common possession of a 'new alphabet'. However, this common experience which they shared then does not mean that they really know how to spell the letters of the new alphabet today. Neither does it imply that they will be allowed to learn them together, or that the new situation with regard to martyrdom has gained common recognition. Thus, I will first attempt to compare the Protestant attitude to martyrdom with that of the Catholic, and then ask of both which special features mark the new type of martyr of whom we are talking.

I. HISTORY

In contrast to Catholic practice, Protestants generally exclude martyrs from their thoughts. They seldom preach about them, and on special days of remembrance, even if conscious of the problem, they are at a loss to know what to say. Furthermore, there seems to be no guidance on the subject forthcoming from theological faculties and church leaders. People are either not sure what is legitimate, or they are already convinced that the names of martyrs should not even be mentioned. It would appear that both contemporary heretics and orthodox Christians put a higher value on their encounter with theology, theory and teaching than they do on their knowledge about or experience of distinguished people and their fate. For a long time there has been a deep-rooted mistrust of anything that looked like the worship of men, and the fear of regarding great men as examples has acted as a brake and a hindrance in acknowledging their significance. We prefer to talk about prophecy rather than prophets. Thus, in comparison with their place in the Roman Catholic and Anglican traditions, theological textbooks enjoy a much higher esteem amongst Protestants than do biographies of great Christians. Protestants may occasionally sing the praises of the 'dear martyrs' in the Te Deum, but we really only take notice of the professors of theology! In the local parishes martyrs are regarded simply as teaching material for the Sunday School and confirmation class, and thus have become stylized, marginal phenomena without any real identity. In the light of all this, it is understandable why experiments with new calendars of the saints and martyrs remain the property of special groups, and are regarded with mistrust by the Church as a whole; and why Protestant encyclopaedias say nothing about martyrdom in modern history.

Why is there this Protestant reaction to martyrdom? Is it because of sound teaching, modesty, or just narrow-mindedness?

Modesty would be a good reason. When in Tegel prison, Bonhoeffer refused to speak about Christian suffering precisely for this reason: 'Perhaps we've made too much of this question of suffering, and been too solemn about it. I've sometimes been surprised that the Roman Catholics take so little notice of that kind of thing. Is it because they're stronger than we are? Perhaps they know better from their own history what suffering and martyrdom really are, and are silent about petty inconveniences and obstacles.'[3]

Of course, the suffering of the martyrs has not completely disappeared from the Protestant tradition, as we can see from some of the popular hymns which are sung. The Augsburg Confession in the sixteenth century even instructs Protestants to 'remember' the martyrs and saints by giving thanks for them, and by gaining strength from their example. However, at the very same time, the Protestant rejection of any Catholic custom which they regarded as a threat to the centrality of Christ and his saving work resulted in a negative attitude towards martyrdom. In other words, this negative approach was regarded as 'sound teaching', and it had a far greater influence than the positive approach of the Lutheran Confession. Doctrine and admonition has thus stood in the way of any direct encounter with the martyrs, preventing their testimony from being known in its creative freedom.

But 'sound teaching' on martyrdom is only half the problem. There is also the emotional struggle which surrounds the history of martyrs, and especially that which has arisen out of the conflict between Catholics and Protestants. This history, which both binds them together and separates them, can be described briefly in terms of five main periods. The first period does not really belong to either, but they have always honoured it as an *exemplum*, which was solely for them. This period is that of the classical form of martyrdom as described in 2 Maccabees, chapter 7, the martyrdom of faithful Jews at the hands of the Roman power. The second period is that of the early Christian Church, with its many martyrs. This martyrology provided, almost exclusively, the material for teaching the arts and for the hymnology of the

Church in the Middle Ages. Indeed, it was because of the extravagant local cults, pilgrimages, calendars and relics associated with these martyrs that the Reformers reacted so negatively to the phenomenon of martyrdom.

A third and frightful period followed – the period of confessional martyrs, victims of the struggle between Catholics and Protestants. It is rather strange that we have so often failed, as we think about this period, to realize how terrible and intense the long period of Jewish martyrdom in Europe has been. We have been preoccupied with the confessional martyrs, and have suppressed the reality of Jewish martyrdom at the hands of Christians. But from the time of the Reformation, Protestants have honoured their martyrs, whom the Catholics burnt at the stake, and Catholics have honoured their martyrs, whom Protestants put to death!

The terrible period of confessional martyrdom was followed by another period during which Catholics and Protestants did not kill each other, but competed on the mission-field for the honour of a martyr's death. For centuries converts of both confessions have suffered for their faith, but Catholics and Protestants have taken very little notice of each other in this regard, and they have seldom if ever admitted the power of the witness of those martyrs of the opposite confession.

But we are now on the threshold of a new understanding in the long history of Christian martyrology. After a period of fighting each other, then a period of ignoring each other, the time has now been ushered in when Catholics and Protestants have begun to experience martyrdom in partnership. Before his cruel death in Nazi Germany, the Jesuit priest Alfred Delp entreated his Protestant fellow-prisoners: 'Attend to it that both our Churches, though not united, no longer shame our common Lord. We have done so for too long. It must come to an end.' In the name of Christ, witnesses of both confessions have sacrificed themselves together for the sake of humanity, and with this a new era has begun. Their authority compels us, not to deny their witness, but to learn the letters of the 'new alphabet' together. This task is already blessed with the seal of their martyrdom, but it also brings with it a new problem which we now have to face.

2. CONTEMPORARY MARTYRDOM

The new problem has arisen because contemporary martyrdom has shifted the emphasis in martyrdom. Whereas formerly martyrdom was the result of bearing testimony to the name of Jesus Christ in a hostile world, now martyrdom is often the result of bearing testimony on behalf of a threatened '*humanum*', it has become a sacrifice for the sake of humanity. And it is not so easy any more to recognize modern martyrs because to do this requires the decoding of the new alphabet, as well as an interpretation of it, with all the preferences and rejections which this implies. The problem becomes clearer when we ask the question: What is the relation between contemporary martyrdom, which results from solidarity with the oppressed, and classical martyrdom in the Maccabean or early Christian sense? Is the modern kind still identical with that of a John Hus or a Thomas More? Martyrdom certainly still occurs in modern times. During the Third Reich, for example, there were the deaths of Protestant pastor Paul Schneider and Catholic priest Josef Metzger at the hands of the Nazis. But what about those who were martyrs because of their solidarity with outcasts and guilty people, men and women like Henri Perrin and Simone Weil? Or those who conspired against Hitler, like Father Delp, Count von Moltke, and Dietrich Bonhoeffer?

At this point our judgement falters. We Protestants still lack the necessary categories which would enable us to deal with this kind of phenomenon. The Lutheran Bishop Meiser refused to attend a remembrance service for Bonhoeffer in Flossenbürg because, as he said, Bonhoeffer was only a political and not a Christian martyr. Even Heinrich Forck, a representative of the provisional leadership of the Confessing Church during the Third Reich, stated the following in a book of commemoration in 1949:

It [true Christian martyrdom] differs from the resistance movement in that the point of departure lay not in politics but only
in the witness of the Church. Everyone mentioned in this book,
and additionally, all the men and women who were under the
same oppression and temptation, took their sufferings upon
them not because they disagreed with the politics of the Third
Reich, recognizing doom for our nation therein, but only and
exclusively because they saw the confession of the Church was
being attacked, and that they had to preserve it for the sake of
Christ, even if it meant risking their lives.[4]

How painfully clear is the separation of the witness of the Church
from the political doom of the people! How fatal is the use of the
word 'political' when reserved, as here, for the rulers while forbidden to the Christian! How awkward is the little word 'only'
in Forck's statement! What is this exclusive confession of the
Church to which he refers and which was defended at such a
high price? Has the Gospel nothing to say about the suffering
caused by the politicians of the Third Reich?

Clearly, the deeds and sufferings of the saints have not yet
created a new alphabet as far as this kind of utterance is concerned. If this is right, then men like Bonhoeffer have only crept
into this book of commemoration by mistake. I suggest we look
more deeply into the matter from five perspectives, on the basis
of which such men and women are given their proper rank as
Christian martyrs. These perspectives come largely from those
standards regarded as valid by the early Church, which, when they
are combined with the circumstances of our present day, gain a
new image and are expressed with fresh power.

Freely chosen suffering

There are those who, because of Auschwitz, object to regarding
Christians who have died at the hands of the Third Reich as
martyrs. In the light of this Jewish passion, which so transcends
imagination, every Christian word is reduced to silence. Thus,
in our search for understanding of contemporary martyrdom the

following criterion must be applied: if those whose martyrdom we want to commemorate cannot be related to this Jewish travail, then we would be well advised to refrain from claiming any universal meaning for them.

And yet, we can learn something very special about the few modern Christian martyrs from this monstrous annihilation and suffering of the Jews. Those who died in Auschwitz were victims. Their birth and name alone made them such, and it did not matter what they did or did not do. Robbed of their right to live, without the possibility of escape, they existed collectively for the sake of being extinguished. However, those modern martyrs about whom we are speaking were free to choose, and their suffering was based on their own decision. They could have collaborated with the authorities, withdrawn from the scene, or fled, and thus they could have survived. Indeed, they could have justified a retreat or exile on the basis of Christian tradition. And so we have to ask whether or not their martyrdom was really necessary, whether it was after all required of them that they step out of line. Further, we have then to ask ourselves whether it would be necessary for us. Whatever our response to these questions, the fact is that they could have acted differently, while the victims of Auschwitz could not, and the fact that they did what they did gives their martyrdom its character of free choice and consent.

There are deaths which bear witness to death, and those which attest to life. Death in terms of Auschwitz is full of destructive accusation; it overwhelmingly proclaims the denial of the '*humanum*'. But the free choice of death as a victim proclaims the future of the '*humanum*', however ambiguous and weak. When all faith seemed to be destroyed, strangled to death, a sign of hope, however vulnerable, was born. Thus, Auschwitz and Warsaw confront and accuse us, while there is consolation in the deaths of men like Delp and von Moltke. In their case, they have freely chosen their responsibility, and as a result their martyrdom has been raised to the level of a creative declaration of faith. It is because of this element of choice that this type of death differs from senseless murder, depressing accidents, the Vietnamese or Nigerian destruction, and also from the senseless and accusing elimination of the Jews.

Death at the hands of others

The early Christians well knew how to distinguish between the freely chosen sacrifice and the self-inflicted martyrdom, and for them this distinction was important. Indeed, they warned against the longing for martyrdom which flourished during the first few centuries. This old distinction still divides Christian martyrdom from every other respectable and heroic martyrdom.

It is unnecessary to deny that joyous and heroic sacrifices have been made for noble ideas, or for political and patriotic ideals. We do not even need to play down the fact that relatively innocent people ran into hostile machine-gun fire and sacrificed themselves with a fanatical salute to Hitler, the man they believed could fulfil their dreams. But such as these had the support and consent of their nation, as well as the applause of their idol in their hour of death. True Christian martyrs, however, undergo the agony of universal rejection. Public disgrace sends them out into physical and psychological isolation. Silent and misunderstood, they allow themselves to be devoured, and commend themselves to God without any other attempt at justification. No public opinion, no applause, relieves the ambiguity of their end.

Martyrs such as these have only arrived at their decision after a long journey, during which they have often tried to evade the issue, although, having made the decision, they realize they should have made it earlier. Some of them, like Bonhoeffer, had serious thoughts about their role, which later appeared to them as providing a way of escape from their necessary task, and which therefore could not be accepted. Even then, they sought places and opportunities where they could make better use of their own personal talents and desires. But finally, they knew when and decided where and how to act. Not until then did their real martyrdom begin, and it was not for an idea or idol, but for the sake of a justified '*humanum*'. And when their martyrdom came to pass, it did so in the twilight of political conspiracy, and under the stifling feeling that their effort had come too late. Certainly, it did not lead to a public confession in the market-place or the Colosseum, nor any obviously heroic notion. Everything took place in the silent incognito of concentration camps and dark cellars.

Solidarity in guilt

The criterion of the acceptance of historical and contemporary guilt distinguishes the new martyrs most clearly from those of the traditional pattern. The background to this new criterion is the history of the Churches themselves, a history in which they have turned a blind eye to the political situation, either by avoiding the issues or by being disloyal to the decisions which they have in fact made. Disappointed and shocked by this weakness and impotence on the part of the Churches, some Christians and church officials eventually decided to become classified with both Christians and non-Christians by involving themselves in the masquerade of a conspiracy. They did so, not only to free the consciences of their companions in the conspiracy, but also in order to share completely in their deeds and fate.

Bonhoeffer had tried three times to flee from his own destiny, as we have already seen. In 1933 he was in clerical exile in London; in 1939 in academic exile in New York; in 1944 he disappeared underground in the conspiracy. But he also returned three times. In 1935 he returned to his persecuted Confessing Church, and wrote:

> We should tell the devil that Jesus has called to himself not the righteous but sinners, and that we – in defiance of the devil – wish to remain sinners in order to be with Jesus rather than be righteous with the devil.[5]

In 1939 he returned to work with his conspiring friends. He then wrote:

> If any man tries to escape guilt in responsibility he detaches

himself from the ultimate reality of human existence, and what is more he cuts himself off from the redeeming mystery of Christ's bearing guilt without sin and he has no share in the divine justification which lies upon this event.[6]

In 1944 he returned to the company of the condemned, and afterwards wrote about Jonah's flight:

'Cast me away! My guilt must bear the wrath of God;
the righteous shall not perish with the sinners!'
They trembled. But with hands that knew no weakness
they cast the offender from their midst. The sea stood still.[7]

Similar acts, though on a different level, were performed by witnesses such as Simone Weil and Henri Perrin.

Thus a new type of martyr has emerged. No longer is he the holy, heroic martyr, but one who is a dishonoured witness on behalf of humanity. He does not distance himself from the world as an example of purity, but stays and shares with those who are involved in the hopes and wrong-doings of this world. It is just here, however, that the Churches have the greatest difficulty in following what has happened in the transformation of the pattern of martyrdom. It seems to them that the possibility of disappearing into a discredited incognito is too great, and that for Christians to appear to have discarded their Christian identity can only be a cause for misunderstanding.

Authentic Christian character
Is it, after all, only evidence of compromise and complicity, when Christians act in this way? Or is it, rather, an act committed in solidarity with Christ himself? This leads us to the fourth perspective, which, in an important sense, is the most basic.

Bonhoeffer wrote in 1940 that the Church had become 'guilty of the deaths of the weakest and most defenceless brothers of Jesus Christ'.[8] Those anxious for the proper maintenance of Christian identity would have liked to see in this solidarity with Christ the fulfilment of a theological obligation. But for the modern martyrs themselves, the realization that the *'humanum'* is the aim and truth of the message of Christ was much more of a disconcerting discovery and release. Thus they hardly ever stressed the fact that they were Christians, and their identity as Christians was never used by them in order to demonstrate anything. For them, this just could not be. Thus, at the precise point where the secret of these martyrs is strongest, we must speak about it most cautiously. Many of them have, nevertheless, in the midst of their identification with the 'weakest brothers of Christ', preserved their Christian identity without boasting about it, and even willingly allowed the possibility of being misunderstood. Indeed, it is not our right to judge them, in any case; they judge us! This means that we must not try and change their witness; they are given to us in order to transform us.

The authority of their death
We must not allow our ideas about these modern martyrs and their character to twist the facts. The validity and authority of their death are not dependent upon our categories and criticisms, nor on our perspectives. On the contrary, their death has become an authentic example and pattern; it has given authority to their testimony for the '*humanum*', and this is a very different authority from that which could be given by synodical decisions and official authorization. Their authority is to be considered and honoured because they have, by their sacrifice, sealed something final and unambiguous, which would otherwise remain ambiguous and capable of falling away. They are 'with Christ' for good, and their authority requires no support and help, or criticism and control. It expresses itself completely in the power of humiliation. And it is this which can become creative for us.

Throughout the centuries there have been intense debates about whether the messenger or the message is most important for the Church. Usually it was decided that everything depended upon the proclamation, and that this was not to be made dependent upon its weak messengers. As long as we live, our words remain ambiguous. But martyrs have always been regarded in a different way. The Church raised them to join the ranks of the apostles and prophets, because in them proclamation and prophet were inseparably joined, each binding the other with an eternal seal. Their words have been substantiated by the language of their deeds. And now, for the sake of Christ, the herald will never again be able to revoke or corrupt his proclamation on behalf of the '*humanum*'. The authority of his testimony has been secured by his death.

And so a new alphabet for the truth of the Gospel has been given to us, in order that we can learn its letters. Witness and testimony for Christ's '*humanum*' have been joined so intensely that they can destroy self-will and create a new understanding. Kierkegaard once wrote about the power of martyrdom:

> In order to win back eternity, blood will have to be claimed, but a different sort of blood; not that of thousands of murdered victims killed by thousands of ways; no, by the valuable blood of individuals, of martyrs. Those who have died so nobly can do what no living person who has killed men by the thousands can do; and what they could not do while alive, they can do when dead: namely, to force a raging crowd to obey.[9]

Martyrs need to be received and acknowledged by us. This is not easily accepted by the Churches; instead the struggle about them continues. I have made certain proposals, but we will have to decide one day for ourselves and thereby determine our own future. Otherwise we will help create another situation in which the painful, lonely sacrifice of new martyrs will be required again. The Spanish philosopher Santayana once said that 'those who do not remember the past are condemned to go through it again'. Thus martyrdom is as valid for us today as it was in former times. Martyrs are there to be honoured and remembered for the sake of new life. And new life in Christ's name, as they have shown, is possible today with a new humanity, interpreting Christ's presence as a crying out and acting on behalf of the humanity of man.

APPENDIX

A Confessing Church in South Africa?

Conclusions from a Visit

I

'Are we involved in a "church struggle" like that in the Third Reich and do we have to create a "Confessing Church" as you did in Germany?' This question was raised in almost every discussion I had in South Africa. The term 'Confessing Church' is indeed current in South Africa today and excites and troubles friend and foe alike. In many quarters the view is that a *status confessionis* now exists, and some individual Christians sacrifice themselves to draw public attention to this fact.

An Anglican priest, David Russell, achieved fame by living for more than six months on the income which blacks in his 'homeland' congregation who receive public assistance are expected to live on, keeping his bishop and member of parliament informed of the course of his 'fast'.[1] With eight members of other denominations, Russell organized a four-week walk from Grahamstown to Cape Town, a distance of a thousand kilometres, holding meetings and services on the way.[2] The Lutherans took no part. Afrikaans-speaking Reformed Church people refused to engage in 'demonstrations'. The object was to draw public attention to the destructiveness of the system introduced by the legislation on migrant labour.[3] This legislation attempted to solve the contradictions inherent in the daily realities of the apartheid system by confining as far as possible all black Africans to the 'homelands' while allowing male Africans to take one-year work contracts, accommodating them (and keeping them under control) in temporary camps in the neighbourhood of the large urban centres, encircled by a sort of no-man's-land, and separated from their wives and children. It would be a travesty to call this system a 'guest-worker system' (*Gastarbeiter-System*).

A Catholic geologist who had taken an African woman into his household so that she could live with her husband, who was working in Johannesburg on a migrant-labour contract, deliberately chose to go to prison rather than pay a few rand to escape the charge against him when the authorities refused to grant the wife permission to stay outside her 'homeland'. The officials of important Christian movements decided, after consultation together, not to obey the unreasonable demands of the authorities and of an ever more tightly drawn network of regulations.

An observer from Germany can hardly fail to be impressed by the striking parallels with the Hitler period.

2

To begin with, any meeting of Christians assumes as a matter of course that 'informers' and police spies will be present. These informers may be people who have been intimidated into such a role or who are paid for doing this work – and these people include non-whites, who are very vulnerable; or they may be people who have been asked very politely to accept this role and who feel it their duty to support government policy in a situation of supposedly grave national danger. In some meetings fervent prayers are offered for (and against) such informers, and occasionally one witnesses astonishingly modern cases of exorcism.

Banning and censorship
Then there is the 'banning' system. Under this system, people – blacks more frequently than whites – are 'banned' for five years or more. This means that they are kept under a kind of 'house arrest' and confined to their place of residence; they are forbidden to meet with more than one person other than their family; and their published works may no longer be sold or quoted. No

reasons are given; there is no right of appeal and no open court proceedings.

Who pays any attention to these cases? In the Confessing Church in Germany a system of intercession lists was organized. That has not been developed in South Africa. As in Hitler's Germany, there is widespread fear of being in any way connected with such people. It is true that at the end of February 1973 a storm of protest lasted for weeks in sections of the South African press when sixteen black and white students, including a black African who had founded a trade union, were banned at a time when the strikes in Durban had led to some signs of a relaxation of the rigid regulations in the field of what is called 'petty apartheid'.

Books are placed on an official 'Index' of banned writings and are then removed from libraries and a ban is put on any quotation from them. For example, William Temple's *Christianity and the Social Order* had to be removed from the library of a state university for black Africans. A collection of studies dealing with 'black theology' also had to go. It is no longer legal, therefore, to quote the material it contains showing the attitude of black Africans to their white-dominated Churches or the evidence it provides of the growing determination of black Africans to abandon such institutions. Everyone knows, of course, that the number of separatist church groups is rapidly increasing.

Another parallel with Hitler's Germany is the way in which government measures are justified by appeal to the 'Suppression of Communism' Act which has been on the statute-book since the fifties. By persistent cultivation of the scapegoat mentality, the government ensures that Christians who analyse the situation and issue warnings find themselves branded as the allies of 'communists and terrorists' and castigated as traitors by South African nationalists. On the walls of the Christian institute in Cape Town some night writer has daubed in red the words: 'COMMY PIGS'.

Anyone who exercises his citizenship by making critical comments on public issues exposes himself, therefore, to the charge of betraying the Gospel. In the state schools political discussion is not encouraged. University students in receipt of a government grant prudently refrain from taking part in political demonstrations. 'You are here to learn, not to think' was how someone described a certain black African university receiving considerable financial support from the Government but established on a very selective basis.

In Germany in the late thirties increasingly efficient methods were used to paralyse the activities of unpopular church groups without provoking any public outcry. In South Africa, too, it is possible today to throttle the activities of church groups without outraging freedom by direct measures which attract attention. For example, the law allows black areas to be declared white, and white areas black, overnight, with all the consequences which this carries with it – the transplantation of churches and institutions, and the resulting destruction of human and structural relationships, to say nothing of the elementary burdens imposed on the ordinary individual. Again, groups composed mainly of blacks can be declared black organizations overnight, in which case they lose the right to retain offices and staff in white areas of the city. In fact, the membership of almost all the denominations is predominantly black. Many church organizations, the South African Council of Churches for example, have made it their deliberate policy to have a majority of blacks on their executive bodies. The threat of being declared a black organization hangs over each of them like a sword of Damocles. One hears it said that important church organizations would like to declare themselves black before the authorities get round to doing so, since a bold step of this kind would force not only the Government but even their own constituent groups to adopt much more straightforward positions.

The parallels with Hitler's Germany in the theory and practice of racial superiority are obvious. South African legislation rests on the maxim: 'Never a white under black.' To reinforce this ideology there are the fears engendered by the simple statistical proportions – 4 million whites to 17 million blacks – and the corresponding birth-rates. Racism and the realities of apartheid have a long history in South Africa. And the Churches have been implicated in them not as victims but as accomplices, sanctioning and supporting them. There are black and white Christians who are waiting for something like a Stuttgart Declaration on the part of the South African Churches. The difficulty here is that it is impossible to utter the words without creating new realities.

Even among his white Christian friends the black senses racism in a hundred ways in traditional behaviour patterns, as well as in the social structures, and also, of course, he sees their mirror-image in the attitudes of the humiliated Africans. This has seldom been expressed as forcibly as it was by the black Anglican bishop Alphaeus Zulu in his great address at the University of Cape Town in 1972.[4] This address also gives us an inkling of the terrifying consequences which could flow from the crude and subtle humiliations to which black Africans are daily exposed, especially under the migrant-labour system, which breeds hatred and estrangement. (White people can turn a blind eye to the inevitable increase of crime in the sealed townships remote from the beautiful cities.) I was told that about two thousand blacks are punished every day for infringements of the law for which whites cannot be punished (in connection with residence regulations, pass laws and the like).

No one is suggesting, of course, that the practice of white superiority in South Africa rests on a secret plan to destroy one whole section of the nation, as was the case with the racism practised under National Socialism. South Africa is not a totalitarian state in the Nazi sense, though to many it appears that way. Behind the policy of 'separate development' (which is the official name for apartheid) there is undoubtedly a concern based ostensibly on Christian values, concern to develop among blacks a more authentic identity and community, something which is stressed in the propaganda issued by South African embassies, although without any apparent awareness of the intolerably paternalistic and didactic approach it implies.

Finally – and this too is a parallel with Hitler's Germany –

there are the depressing, unending struggles between the different church groups. The dividing lines run not only between whites, coloureds, Asians and blacks, or between the historic denominations but, in addition, between the different immigrant groups, especially between the Afrikaners and the British. The group faith, insulated as by an iron curtain against biblical and ecumenical insights, serves the group internally as a defence against threatened loss of identity amidst so much that is alien, and externally as a vehicle for imposing impossible obligations on the other groups, thus once again reinforcing the group's own self-assurance. The time for declarations of guilt is not even remotely on the horizon here.

An example or a handicap?

But this tends to reduce the faith to a multiplicity of Christian 'tribal religions', as an able Johannesburg theologian put it, tribal faiths to which the immigrant clings in order to survive in the as yet unintegrated new country. We saw something like this happen on a national scale among the German Christians. We know how an inward-turned doctrine of justification can be fused with an intense cult of home and country. But there are in South Africa new variations, terribly efficient in isolating groups and rendering them insensitive to their nearest neighbours and environment, and reinforced by powerful social, economic and military interests. Part of the picture here are the belated mammoth national South African shrines which strike Europeans today as absurd and even tactless. Consider the Voortrekker Memorial in Pretoria, dedicated in 1938, which is built in the monumental style of a national war memorial with a panel in the entrance giving detailed instructions about how visitors should conduct themselves in such a sanctuary.

The edginess of those who reject the validity of such parallels (the list of which is far from complete) and the constant preoccupation of those who mull over the consequences these parallels could have for themselves personally (and who, moreover, look to us in Germany to share in their reflections) clearly show that the drawing of such parallels touches a raw nerve. But how helpful in fact is this example of the Confessing Church?

3

In the first place, the very fact that the term and the picture (in any case an idealized one) of a Confessing Church are there *before* the thing itself has taken shape and become a reality is a handicap and already felt by some to be so. In Germany the reality came first and the name only later. And the name itself came to be used only because of a background of certain traditions which are not everywhere the same. In any thorough enquiry it would certainly be essential to examine these differences in background and to clarify hazy notions about the name 'Confessing Church'.

The most an outside observer can do is to draw attention to certain differences of emphasis. Only those who are directly involved can really decide in favour of a name and the reality it stands for. Direct involvement in South Africa begins with a very costly basic decision, one which it was given to only a very small number of Christians in Germany in 1933 to make, namely, the decision whether or not to stand up to the developments in their country without having any escape clause. In South Africa one frequently meets people who are seriously considering leaving the country – not only those who have foreign citizenship, but even people whose families have been South African for generations.

For the Confessing Church in Germany the rediscovery of the '*solus Christus*' (Christ alone) was a central experience. This '*solus*' challenged appeals then being made in Germany to another 'revelation' and resolutely opposed the attempts of certain German Christians to assimilate the Christian faith through such appeals into some kind of syncretism. The dividing line was clear enough even though many serious theologians and churchmen at that time refused to accept the existence of a *status confessionis*. The confession of this '*solus*' inevitably led to ecclesiological decisions. It produced in 1934 the Barmen Declaration, with its six short articles. It thereby established a certain room to breathe within the prevailing confusion. Because of its rallying force it represented a political factor of some importance for the Hitler regime. In addition, the Christians who confessed their faith in terms of this '*solus Christus*' also bore witness against the biological racism of that time, but they did so only incidentally and not yet, at the time of Barmen, in explicit terms. For the Churches, the 'solution' of the Jewish question was for a long time no more than a marginal problem. Other tasks seemed to them to be more important and more central.

In South Africa today many people, whether they support or oppose this or any other kind of apartheid, are at one in appealing to this '*solus Christus*' of the Reformation. Prime Minister Vorster appealed to pastors to return to the heart of their message and to preach the word of God and the Gospel of Christ to their congregations. That is a measure of the confusion that exists today in South Africa. Which of the Western countries has a government which still appeals so explicitly to the Christian faith? Certainly the Nationalists are not against organized religion, nor would they easily tolerate the *Führerprinzip* in their party or the Church.

The difficulty of practising unity

In South Africa the rallying cry is '*Unitas*', the unity of the Body of Christ. This is the great theme – unity and the form unity should take. But it is so in quite a different way from that in which it is generally understood in ecumenical circles. The theme is a much more urgent and costly one in this society riven by denominational, sectarian, historical, cultural, ethnic and racial divisions which provides such fertile soil for apartheid legislation designed to shore up a labour-repressive society of long standing in which it is not the private citizen who has access to a reservoir of cheap labour (as it was in Rome) but a whole society.

The *unitas* of the Body of Christ is as clear in theory as it is difficult in practice, and there is disagreement about the existence of a *status confessionis* at this point. The breathing-space this unity provides is as welcome to some as it is alarming to others. In fact, however seldom it happens and however tentatively, it is almost only in the Churches that people divided by law into the privileged and the unprivileged actually eat together at the same table, stay under the same roof, and sometimes even confer together under the chairmanship of a black African, or that a coloured bishop confirms white Christians within a diocese which includes black townships.

But what prospect is there of a South African 'Barmen' over the issue of the *unitas* of the Body of Christ and the form this *unitas* should take? A whole series of important documents in recent years base their arguments on the biblical principle of *unitas*; for example, the declarations made by the South African Council of Churches in 1968, 1972 and March 1973.[5] These were not enough, however, to produce an event comparable to Barmen 1934: a synod's declaration and its acceptance by congregations, resulting eventually in an organized, identifiable Confessing Church. Authoritative declarations separating from some and declaring solidarity with others, meant to provide criteria for distinguishing between true and false church leadership, and indicating which is the right way to go and which not, have not been issued. Barmen drove us towards a reconstituted church leadership and led to changes producing regroupings in matters of church finance, administration and training. This was possible because there still existed a tradition of thinking and working in the monolithic categories of a single confessional church structure, so that it came more naturally to us to accept an authoritative church leadership from above than a diffuse popular church basis in the individual congregations.

The South African Council of Churches, however, is not an authoritative court of the Church but only a loose federation which cannot and is not expected to make decisions for the Churches and congregational bodies which make up its membership. It can exercise influence only by the excellence of its work, and this it does. But it deals with specific issues as they arise and does not exercise any permanent authority. The basis here is the denominational system, which precludes in principle any attempt to settle denominational conflicts. This makes it extremely difficult to apply the example of the Confessing Church. Where is there any room here for taking decisions concerning the true Church and the false or for declaring the existence of a *status confessionis*?

The Churches in South Africa have never been regional or national Churches, nor national confessional Churches in our German sense. Someone maliciously suggested that they distinguish between truth and heresy only in the competition for new members. That would perhaps be more applicable to conditions in America; yet position, race, date of foundation, country of origin, number of members, and social desirability do make congregations in South Africa into independent social groups rather than confessional congregations. Even among the Lutherans it is proving difficult to overcome this 'localism', for example, in the efforts to unite groups of Lutheran Churches in Transvaal, Natal, Cape Province and South West Africa. Indeed, it threatens to bring even these very confessionally-minded Christians to the very brink of complete separation.

Over against this difference in traditional background, however, there is one other important factor: an unmistakable common responsibility for the political dimension of the confession of the *unitas* of the Body of Christ and for its practical application, still possible though fraught with danger.

In the German church struggle the confession of the '*solus Christus*' was not extended to include the area of the political struggle for the '*humanum*'. Such an extension was not intended nor considered. Whatever the reasons may have been, whether it was possible or not, the fact is that the Confessing Church, though a political factor of some magnitude, was not politically activist. This stepped up the price of responsible partnership in creating a different society in Germany to such a degree that certain members of the Confessing Church found they could only discharge that responsibility by joining in the plot against Hitler, with all its heavy consequences.

In South Africa, however, the confession of the unity of the

Body of Christ extends in the first place to the concept of the 'multiracial Church'. This 'multiracial Church' proves itself to be such by its congregational life, its organization, its appointment of ministers and other offices, its training, its planning, its financial responsibility, its allocation of resources. Such a multiracial Church is obviously inconceivable without the political dimension of possible concepts of a multiracial society, or without frank acceptance of political struggle to achieve such a society by all democratic means. Here there is an astonishing alliance of forces: between the various sections of the parliamentary opposition, the small Progressive Party of Helen Suzman and Colin Eglin, and, above all, a remarkably outspoken English-language press, and even some very influential industrialists – allies whom we in the Third Reich could not even have dreamt of having. Political responsibility for the *'humanum'* forms an integral element in declarations such as those issued by the South African Council of Churches.

The Lutheran visitor from Germany is somewhat surprised, of course, to find a false separation between the 'two kingdoms' widely held in all denominations. It is such a ready-made alibi. Even in opposition circles people have allowed their use of the word 'politics' to be dictated by popular usage. They are rather too anxious to assure you that they are not thinking in terms of politics, forgetting how political this would make them – and in what sense – if it were true. Superficial arguments, supposedly based on the Bible, give countenance to the idea that the Government and the party politicians, in virtue of their special public responsibilities, also control all political activities.

Yet the fact that people in South Africa are talking about a 'Confessing Church' shows how deeply they realize that they cannot stand for a multiracial Church unless at the same time they work openly together for a multiracial society and that they would become hopeless accomplices of this apartheid society if they were to retreat to some imagined third, neutral position, in which, instructed by the 'Church', they would keep quiet about political matters.

Pessimistic voices are heard. Someone asserts that the next elections will be the last, to be followed by open military dictatorship. A frequent visitor from England observes that the black Africans have become much more aware of themselves than they were two years ago but that the political scene has darkened considerably. In actual fact the homeland leaders are cleverly exploiting the apartheid system to promote the true interests of black Africans and people are talking of the possibility of apartheid becoming a Trojan horse within white society. Is there still time? Is dialogue between blacks and whites still possible? Certainly in many places in the South African Churches the answer is 'Yes'.

NOTES

INTRODUCTION: THE RESPONSE TO BONHOEFFER

1. E. Bethge, *Dietrich Bonhoeffer* (Collins, London, and Harper & Row, New York, 1970).
2. *Voprosy Filizofii*, no. 2 (1968), pp. 94–102.
3. *Honest to God* (SCM Press, London, and Westminster Press, Philadelphia, 1963).
4. *Sanctorum Communio* (E.T., Collins, London, 1963), published in the USA under the title *The Communion of Saints* (Harper & Row, New York, 1963).
5. *Act and Being* (E.T., Collins, London, and Harper, New York, 1962).
6. *Letters and Papers from Prison* (E.T., SCM Press, London, and Macmillan, New York, enlarged and revised edition, 1971; first English edition published in 1953).
7. *Church Dogmatics*, vol. IV, part 2 (E.T., T. & T. Clark, Edinburgh, and Charles Scribner's Sons, New York, 1958), p. 641.
8. *The Cost of Discipleship* (E.T., SCM Press, London, and Macmillan, New York, 1959).
9. *Life Together* (E.T., SCM Press, London, and Harper, New York, 1954).
10. *Letters and Papers from Prison*, p. 369.
11. H. Müller, *Von der Kirche zur Welt* (Herbert Reich Ev. Vlg., Hamburg-Bergstadt, 1961).
12. H. Ott, *Wirklichkeit und Glaube* (Vandenhoek & Ruprecht, Zürich, 1966; E.T., Lutterworth, London, 1972).
13. Published in D. Bonhoeffer, *The Way to Freedom*, vol. II of E.T. of *Gesammelte Schriften* (Collins, London, and Harper & Row, New York, 1966), p. 116. See notes 30 and 31.
14. *Church Dogmatics*, vol. IV, part 2, pp. 533f.
15. *Ethics* (E.T., SCM Press, London, and Macmillan, New York, 1971).
16. *The New Man* (SCM Press, London, 1956).
17. cf. *Ethics*, pp. 161ff.
18. cf. E. Wolf, in *Die Mündige Welt*, vol. IV, ed. E. Bethge (Chr. Kaiser Verlag, Munich, 1963).
19. *The Promise of Bonhoeffer* (Lippincott, Philadelphia, 1969).
20. *Ethics in a Christian Context* (SCM Press, London, and Harper & Row, New York, 1963).
21. Published in *Evangelische Theologie*, no. 10 (October 1968), p. 556; E.T. in

K. Barth, *Fragments Grave and Gay* (Collins, Fontana, London, 1971), p. 122.

22. Published in *Word and Faith* (SCM Press, London, and Fortress Press, Philadelphia, 1963).

23. Published in English as *The Future of Our Religious Past* (SCM Press, London, and Harper & Row, New York, 1971).

24. See Harbsmeier's article, 'Die "nicht-religiöse Interpretation biblischer Bergriffe" bei Bonhoeffer und die Entmythologisierung', in *Die Mündige Welt*, vol. II, ed. E. Bethge (1959), pp. 74ff.

25. ibid., vol. III, ed. E. Bethge (1960), pp. 11ff.

26. ibid., vol. IV, p. 33.

27. ibid., vol. III, pp. 42ff.

28. *World Come of Age* (Collins, London, 1967).

29. *Christology* (E.T., Collins, London, and Harper & Row, New York, 1966).

30. *Gesammelte Schriften*, vols. I–VI, ed. E. Bethge (Chr. Kaiser Verlag, Munich, 1958–74).

31. *No Rusty Swords: Letters, Lectures and Notes, 1928–1936* (Collins, London, and Harper & Row, New York, 1965); *The Way to Freedom: Letters, Lectures and Notes, 1935–1939* (Collins, London, and Harper & Row, New York, 1966); *True Patriotism: Letters, Lectures and Notes, 1939–1945* (Collins, London, and Harper & Row, New York, 1973). All volumes edited by E. H. Robertson.

32. See n. 11; J. D. Godsey, *The Theology of Dietrich Bonhoeffer* (SCM Press, London, and Westminster Press, Philadelphia, 1960).

33. 'Bonhoeffer, Christology and Ethic United', in *Christianity and Crisis*, vol. XXIV, no. 17 (1964), p. 195.

34. The first substantial book by a Roman Catholic scholar is Ernst Feil's *Die Theologie Dietrich Bonhoeffers: Hermeneutik-Christologie-Weltverständnis* (Chr. Kaiser Verlag, Munich, 1971).

35. *Reality and Faith*, p. 24.

BONHOEFFER IN SOUTH AFRICA

1. In *Commonweal* (17 September 1965), p. 657.

2. J. A. Phillips, *The Form of Christ in the World* (Collins, London, 1967), published in the USA under the title *Christ for Us in the Theology of Dietrich Bonhoeffer* (Harper & Row, New York, 1967), p. 23.

3. *The Cost of Discipleship*, p. 79.

4. cf. *Gesammelte Schriften*, vol. VI, ed. E. Bethge (1974), p. 260. (our translation). See also L. Rasmussen, *Dietrich Bonhoeffer: Reality and Resistance* (Abingdon, Nashville, 1972), p. 218.

5. *Frontier*, vol. 17, no. 2 (Summer 1974), p. 66.
6. cf. 'After Ten Years', in *Letters and Papers from Prison*, esp. p. 17.
7. ibid., pp. 15f.
8. E. Bethge, *Dietrich Bonhoeffer*, p. 693.
9. In a newspaper interview given during the South African Congress on Mission and Evangelism, Durban, March 1973.
10. cf. P. Hinchliff, *The Church in South Africa* (S.P.C.K., London, 1968); J. M. Sales, *The Planting of the Churches in South Africa* (Eerdmans, Grand Rapids, 1971); E. Strassberger, *Ecumenism in South Africa, 1936–1960* (SACC, Johannesburg, 1974); J. W. de Gruchy, 'Reflections on Dialogue between the Afrikaans and English-speaking Churches', in the *Ned. Geref. Teologiese Tydskrif*, vol. XV, no. 2 (March 1974), pp. 120ff.
11. cf. *Sanctorum Communio*, pp. 144f.
12. *Ethics*, p. 94.
13. From 'Night Voices in Tegel', in *Letters and Papers from Prison*, p. 353.
14. cf. M. Wilson, 'Is B.O.S.S. Afraid of Free and Open Encounter?', in *South African Outlook* (October 1972), p. 168.
15. cf. *Sanctorum Communio*, pp. 83, 114.
16. *Ethics*, pp. 64–5.
17. *Letters and Papers from Prison*, pp. 382f.
18. *Apartheid and the Church*, Spro-cas Church Report (Spro-cas Publications, Johannesburg, 1972).
19. ibid., p. 69.
20. M. Buthelezi, 'Six Theses: Theological Problems of Evangelism in the South African Context', in *Journal of Theology for Southern Africa*, no. 3 (June 1973), p. 55.
21. Bonhoeffer declared that 'only he who cries out for the Jews may also sing the Gregorian chant'. Quoted in H. Zahrnt, 'Der Gefangene von Tegel', in *Sontagsblatt* (10 April 1955), p. 1; cf. *Ethics*, pp. 62ff.
22. The Cottesloe Consultation was held in Johannesburg in December 1960. Arranged under the auspices of the World Council of Churches, it was a consultation of the South African member Churches, which then included the Dutch Reformed Church, on the subject of race relations. cf. *Cottesloe Consultation* (Johannesburg, 1961).
23. cf. J. W. de Gruchy and W. B. de Villiers (eds.), *The Message in Perspective* (SACC, Johannesburg, 1968).
24. cf. J. S. Conway, *The Nazi Persecution of the Churches, 1933–45* (Weidenfeld & Nicolson, London, and Basic Books, New York, 1968).
25. cf. H. Adam, *Modernizing Racial Domination: The Dynamics of South African Politics* (University of California Press, Berkeley, California, 1971), esp. ch. 3. A much more strident view was taken in 'An Open Letter con-

cerning Nationalism, National Socialism and Christianity', supplement to *Pro Veritate* (July 1971).

26. 'Confessing the Faith in Japan', in *The South East Asia Journal of Theology* (July–October 1966), p. 161.

27. The Lutheran Church in South Africa is divided into a number of regional synods (black) and a white German-speaking synod. After a lengthy period of negotiation for union between them, the black synods decided they could wait no longer for their white counterparts, and are in the process of uniting without them. The issue is clearly a racial rather than a confessional or theological one.

28. These Churches are all multiracial in composition, with the exception of two of the three Presbyterian Churches involved. The Bantu and the Tsonga Presbyterian Churches are black Churches which have come from Scottish and Swiss missions. In 1973 the Churches agreed to a Declaration of Intention to Seek Union.

29. See Rasmussen, *Dietrich Bonhoeffer: Reality and Resistance*, for a discussion on this issue.

30. *No Rusty Swords*, p. 326.

31. cf. Bonhoeffer's correspondence in *No Rusty Swords*, pp. 250ff.; and for the correspondence between the South African Council of Churches, and the member Churches of the World Council in South Africa, and Geneva, see *Pro Veritate*, vol. IX, no. 6 (October 1970), vol. X, no. 3 (July 1971). See also the *Ecumenical Review*, vol. 25, no. 2 (1971).

32. 'The Challenge of Dietrich Bonhoeffer's Life and Theology', in the Chicago Theological Seminary *Register*, vol. LI, no. 2 (February 1961), p. 3.

33. *The Way to Freedom*, pp. 240f.

34. cf. *Letters and Papers from Prison*, pp. 370f.

35. ibid., pp. 280f., *et al.*

36. There is a growing literature on these issues within South Africa. cf., *inter alia*, M. Motlhabi (ed.), *Essays on Black Theology* (University Christian Movement, Johannesburg, 1972), published in Great Britain under the title *Black Theology: South African Voice*, ed. B. Moore (Hurst, London, 1974), and in the USA under the title *The Challenge of Black Theology in South Africa*, ed. B. Moore (John Knox Press, Atlanta, 1974); H. J. Becken (ed.), *Relevant Theology for Africa* (Lutheran Publishing House, Durban, 1973); and D. J. Bosch, *Het Evangelie in Afrikaans Gewaad* (J. H. Kok, Kampen, 1974), an excellent account of the overall situation by a South African Dutch Reformed theologian.

37. *No Rusty Swords*, p. 160. See *Letters and Papers from Prison*, p. 281, *et al.*

38. Quoted by Bethge in *Dietrich Bonhoeffer*, p. 38.

Notes

I. CREDIBLE MINISTRY

1. Letter of 2.2.1934, quoted in *Dietrich Bonhoeffer*, pp. 22f.
2. *Sanctorum Communio*, p. 157.
3. ibid., p. 161.
4. ibid., p. 153.
5. In letters to friends, *Gesammelte Schriften*, vol. I, pp. 78, 24.
6. cf. *Act and Being*, p. 142. The English translation in the 1962 edition (Collins and Harper) omits the following: 'in the strength of the faith of the congregation, *not* in', after 'the strength of Christ', which completely contradicts what Bonhoeffer said.
7. *Gesammelte Schriften*, vol. I, p. 26; vol. III, p. 30.
8. *Dietrich Bonhoeffer*, pp. 154f.
9. *Gesammelte Schriften*, vol. I, pp. 33f.
10. *Dietrich Bonhoeffer*, p. 129.
11. *Gesammelte Schriften*, vol. I, p. 63.
12. ibid., vol. I, p. 31.
13. ibid., vol. II, p. 39.
14. ibid., vol. I, p. 40.
15. *The Cost of Discipleship*, pp. 175f.
16. ibid., p. 186.
17. i.e. the 'illegal' preachers' seminary of which Bonhoeffer was director on behalf of the Confessing Church during 1936–7. Finkenwalde is near Stettin on the Baltic coast.
18. Letter of 14.1.1935, in *Gesammelte Schriften*, vol. III, p. 25.
19. ibid., vol. IV, pp. 291f.
20. In a letter to Karl Barth, 19.9.1936, ibid., pp. 284f.
21. From a proposal to the Council of Brethren of the Old Prussian Union Church, 6.7.1935, ibid., vol. II, pp. 448ff.; *Dietrich Bonhoeffer*, p. 385.
22. *Dietrich Bonhoeffer*, pp. 385f.
23. *Gesammelte Schriften*, vol. III, p. 324. This is from a part of the paper which is lost, but which has been reconstructed from extant notes.
24. ibid., vol. IV, pp. 247f.
25. ibid., vol. II, pp. 344f.
26. ibid., vol. IV, pp. 276f.
27. ibid., vol. II, pp. 439ff.
28. See below, p. 151.
29. *Letters and Papers from Prison*, p. 359.

2. A CHURCH OF INTEGRITY

1. *Dietrich Bonhoeffer*, p. 42.
2. From his lecture 'Das Wesen der Kirche', published in the German edition of the biography *Dietrich Bonhoeffer* (Chr. Kaiser Verlag, Munich, 1967), p. 1060, and now in *Gesammelte Schriften*, vol. V, pp. 227-75.
3. ibid., p. 1058.
4. ibid., p. 1065.
5. ibid., p. 1069.
6. ibid., p. 1068.
7. Published in *Evangelische Theologie*, no. 10 (October 1968), p. 555. An English translation of the letter is published in *Fragments Grave and Gay*, pp. 119ff.
8. *No Rusty Swords*, pp. 221ff.
9. Letter of 14.4.1933, in *Gesammelte Schriften*, vol. I, p. 37.
10. *No Rusty Swords*, p. 222.
11. cf. ibid., p. 223.
12. The 'Crystal Night' of 9 November 1938 is infamous in German history as the night during which anti-Semitic terrorism reached a new intensity, with the destruction of synagogues, Jewish shops, etc.
13. *Einheit von Evangelium und Volkstum* (Hamburg, 1933), p. 17.
14. The Barmen Declaration was produced by the Confessing Church at its synod in May 1934 at Barmen. Karl Barth played a major role in its drafting. The Declaration clearly states the basic theological issues behind the church struggle, and proclaims that Jesus Christ alone is God's word to man and the charter of the life and faith of the Church.
15. *Theologische Existenz heute*, new series, 46 (1956), p. 59; cf. Karl Barth, *The German Church Struggle* (E.T., Lutterworth, London, and John Knox Press, Richmond, 1965), p. 75.
16. *Letters and Papers from Prison*, p. 328.
17. *Ethics*, p. 258.
18. ibid., p. 263.
19. ibid.
20. ibid., pp. 266f.
21. *Letters and Papers from Prison*, p. 382.
22. *Evangelische Theologie*, vol. 27 (1967), p. 544.
23. *Letters and Papers from Prison*, pp. 280f.
24. ibid., p. 300.
25. ibid., pp. 360f.

Notes

3. TRUE ECUMENISM

1. *Dietrich Bonhoeffer*, p. 50.
2. *In the Steps of Bonhoeffer*, ed. J. M. Bailey and D. Gilbert (Macmillan, New York, 1969), p. v.
3. Letter of 5.11.1942, in *Gesammelte Schriften*, vol. VI, pp. 557f.
4. *Dietrich Bonhoeffer*, p. 189.
5. *Gesammelte Schriften*, vol. I, pp. 140ff; *No Rusty Swords*, pp. 157ff.
6. *Dietrich Bonhoeffer*, p. 189.
7. *Gesammelte Schriften*, vol. I, p. 144.
8. ibid., p. 145; *No Rusty Swords*, p. 160.
9. *Dietrich Bonhoeffer*, p. 190. I would prefer the word 'authority' to be used instead of 'power'.
10. ibid., p. 184.
11. *In the Steps of Bonhoeffer*, p. vii.
12. *Dietrich Bonhoeffer*, p. 306.
13. *Gesammelte Schriften*, vol. I, p. 240. This paper is published in English translation in *No Rusty Swords*, pp. 326ff.
14. *Gesammelte Schriften*, vol. I, p. 242; *No Rusty Swords*, p. 327.
15. ibid., p. 243; *No Rusty Swords*, p. 328.
16. ibid.; *No Rusty Swords*, pp. 328–9.
17. *A History of the Ecumenical Movement, 1517–1948*, edited by R. Rouse and S. C. Neill (S.P.C.K., London, and Westminster Press, Philadelphia, 1954), p. 583.
18. *Gesammelte Schriften*, vol. I, pp. 244f.; *Dietrich Bonhoeffer*, pp. 400f.
19. *Gesammelte Schriften*, vol. I, p. 248.
20. *Dietrich Bonhoeffer*, p. 294.
21. ibid., p. 466.
22. Dietrich's twin-sister Sabine was married to Gerhard Leibholz who was of Jewish background.
23. *Dietrich Bonhoeffer*, p. 541 (Bonhoeffer's italics).
24. *Gesammelte Schriften*, vol. II, p. 49.
25. *Dietrich Bonhoeffer*, p. 560.
26. *Gesammelte Schriften*, vol. I, p. 315.
27. ibid., pp. 323–54; cf. *No Rusty Swords*, pp. 92ff.
28. *Dietrich Bonhoeffer*, p. 564.
29. ibid.
30. ibid.
31. ibid., p. 565.
32. ibid., pp. 718f.
33. ibid., p. 669.

34. ibid., p. 830.
35. ibid., pp. 833f.

4. THE DILEMMA OF EXILE

1. cf. ch. 2 above, part 2, on 'The Church and Race'.
2. R. C. D. Jasper, *George Bell, Bishop of Chichester* (Oxford University Press, London and New York, 1967), pp. 140, 143.
3. *Gesammelte Schriften*, vol. II, p. 45.
4. Letter of 13.7.1934, in *Gesammelte Schriften*, vol. VI, p. 295.
5. *Gesammelte Schriften*, vol. I, p. 42.
6. ibid., p. 373.
7. ibid., pp. 300, 297f.
8. The direct translation of the German title of *Letters and Papers from Prison: Widerstand und Ergebung*.
9. *Letters and Papers from Prison*, p. 16.

5. CHRISTIAN POLITICAL INVOLVEMENT

1. cf. *Lutherische Monatshefte*, no. 11 (1969), p. 564.
2. *Evangelische Theologie*, vol. 28, no. 10 (October 1968), p. 555; *Fragments Grave and Gay*, pp. 120f.
3. *Gesammelte Schriften*, vol. I, pp. 42f.
4. *Ethics*, pp. 91ff.
5. *Dietrich Bonhoeffer*, p. 525.
6. cf. *Ethics*, pp. 331f.
7. *True Patriotism*, p. 198.
8. cf. *Letters and Papers from Prison*, p. 16.
9. *Dietrich Bonhoeffer*, p. 702.
10. *Letters and Papers from Prison*, p. 129.
11. *Dietrich Bonhoeffer*, p. 700.
12. *Letters and Papers from Prison*, p. 174.
13. *Ethics*, p. 314.
14. ibid., pp. 314f.
15. ibid., pp. 207ff.

6. AUTHENTIC THEOLOGY

1. *Union Seminary Quarterly Review*, vol. XXV, no. 1 (1969), pp. 1–18.
2. cf. *Dietrich Bonhoeffer* (German edition), p. 1049; *Gesammelte Schriften*, vol. V, p. 187.
3. *Letters and Papers from Prison*, pp. 380ff.
4. ibid., p. 378. The quotation marks around 'modern' are Bonhoeffer's own.

5. ibid., pp. 378–9.
6. ibid., p. 384.
7. ibid., p. 383.
8. G. Ebeling, *Word and Faith*, pp. 98ff.
9. *Letters and Papers from Prison*, p. 359.
10. ibid., p. 381.
11. Benjamin A. Reist, *The Promise of Bonhoeffer*, p. 82.
12. *Ethics*, pp. 171f.
13. *Letters and Papers from Prison*, pp. 348f.
14. ibid., p. 381.
15. Mottu, op. cit., p. 11.
16. *Letters and Papers from Prison*, p. 382.
17. cf. ibid., pp. 281, 286, 300.
18. Mottu, op. cit., p. 10.
19. *Letters and Papers from Prison*, p. 382.
20. ibid.
21. ibid., p. 383.
22. ibid., pp. 383, 393.

7. MODERN MARTYRDOM

1. M. Baumgarten, *Ein aus 45-jähriger Erfahrung geschöpfter Beitrag zur Kirchenfrage*, vol. 1 (ed. Studt, Kiel, 1891), title page.
2. *Gesammelte Schriften*, vol. IV, p. 71.
3. *Letters and Papers from Prison*, p. 232.
4. B. H. Forck, 'Und folget ihrem Glauben nach', in *Gedenkbuch für die Blutzeugen der Bekennenden Kirche* (1949), p. 7.
5. *Creation and Temptation* (SCM Press, London, 1966), p. 125; published in the USA under the title *Creation and Fall/Temptation* (Macmillan, New York, 1965).
6. *Ethics*, p. 210.
7. *Letters and Papers from Prison*, p. 399.
8. *Ethics*, p. 93.
9. The original reference has been lost, but cf. *The Journals of Kierkegaard, 1834–1854*, ed. Alexander Dru (Collins, Fontana, London, 1958), p. 151.

APPENDIX: A CONFESSING CHURCH IN SOUTH AFRICA?

1. cf. his letters reprinted in *International Review of Missions*, vol. LXII, no. 247 (July 1973).
2. See *South African Outlook*, January–February 1973.
3. See especially *Migrant Labour in South Africa* by Francis Wilson (Spro-cas

Publications, Johannesburg, 1972).

4. *The Dilemma of a Black South African* (University of Cape Town, Cape Town, 1972).

5. See *The Message in Perspective*, a book about the 'Message to the People of South Africa', edited by J. W. de Gruchy and W. B. de Villiers; *Apartheid and the Church* (Spro-cas Publications, Johannesburg, 1972); in March 1973 the South African Council of Churches refused to give evidence to the Schlebusch Commission, a parliamentary select committee investigating the Christian Institute, the Institute of Race Relations, and the University Christian Movement, on the grounds that it was a non-judicial commission whose proceedings were held in secret.

INDEX OF NAMES

Index of Names